THE DALES W

"SEVEN GLORIOU~ ~~~~~"

A PICTORIAL WALKING GUIDE

**Written and illustrated
by Alistair Wallace**

JEMA PUBLICATIONS

Published 1997 by Jema Publications

© Alistair Wallace

ISBN   1-871468-53-1

Publisher's Note
Every care has been taken in the preparation of this book and all the
information has been carefully checked and is believed to be correct at
the time of publication. However, neither the author not the publishers
can accept responsibility for any errors or omissions or for any loss,
damage, injury or inconvenience resulting from the use of this book.

Jema Publications
40 Ashley Lane
Moulton
Northampton
NN3 7TJ

Printed in Great Britain by Woolnough Bookbinding Ltd., Wellingborough.

ACKNOWLEDGEMENTS

My sincere gratitude goes out to the following people without whom I could not have completed this book.
Mr Rod Morrell, NCS Plc, Ponteland, Newcastle. The staff of NCS, Mr J Wallace, Mrs L Furlong, the staff of the numerous Tourist Information Offices along the route, Mr H C Wallace and finally but certainly not least, the people along The Dales Way who make it what it is.

All maps are based upon the Ordnance Survey Maps and used with permission of The Controller of Her Majesty's Stationery Office, © Crown copyright.

Front cover picture of Kettlewell Village is reproduced from an original watercolour painting by the author.

DEDICATION

This book is dedicated to the memory of my mother "Peggy" and to that of my mother-in-law Sheila.

INTRODUCTION

The Dales Way Walk has been divided into easy to follow sections and although the author spent seven days walking the route it is a relatively simple task to spend longer allowing more time for exploration along the walk.

Each section has a map and accompanying text together with the mileage and difficulty rating. Easy meaning that the terrain is not too difficult and is fairly flat. Moderate meaning that the route is slightly more undulating.

Also within each section are Special Points of Interest; Facilities giving amenities, and Accommodation as listed by The Dales Way Association.

Although the strip maps are a useful guide and every effort has been made to ensure accuracy, there is no substitute for the Ordnance survey maps, which should always be used for map and compass work.

CONTENTS

Acknowledgements and Dedication iii
Introduction iv
Contents v
Foreword 1
Symbols used on the maps 3
The Dales Way Association 4
Preparing for a Walk 5
The Dales Way 11
The Route of The Dales Way 12
Ilkley 13
Ilkley to Addingham 15
Addingham to Bolton Priory 19
Bolton Priory 21
Bolton Priory to Barden Bridge 23
Barden Bridge to Burnsall 26
Burnsall to Grassington 30
Grassington to Conistone Pie 33
Conistone Pie to Kettlewell 36
Kettlewell to Hubberholme 38
Hubberholme 41
Hubberholme to Beckermonds 43
Beckermonds to Cam Houses 45
Cam Houses to Far Gearstones 47
Settle to Carlisle Railway 49
Far Gearstones to Lea Yeat 52
Lea Yeat to Dent 55
Dent 58
Dent to Millthrop Bridge (Sedbergh) 60
Sedbergh 64
Sedbergh to Lincoln's Inn Bridge 65
Lincoln's Inn Bridge to Crook of Lune 67
Crook of Lune to Grayrigg 69
Grayrigg to Burneside 72
Burneside to Staveley 76
Staveley 78

Staveley to Hag End Farm   80
Hag End Farm to Bowness   82
Bowness-on-Windermere   85
Reflections   86
Tribute   87
Index   88

FOREWORD

"The best walk we have done."
"We never knew we had such beautiful countryside on our own doorstep."
"We had seven glorious days."
The comments are endless and all relating to the same long distance walk.

It was in the 1960's that a group from the West Riding Ramblers Association conceived the idea of creating a long distance footpath that would encompass the West Riding of Yorkshire and the County of Westmorland. The route they devised from Ilkley to the shores of Windermere at Bowness would encapture some of the most awesome and conflicting countryside ever seen on such a route, contrasting the riverside splendour of Wharfedale with the magnificent rolling hills of Westmorland.

The walk would have something for everyone. A walk that would appeal to novice and veteran alike, and so in 1968 THE DALES WAY was born.

As with most 'ways' the passing of the years see the walks extended and in this respect The Dales Way is no exception. Whilst there are now three 'link routes' arriving from the more urban conurbations of Leeds, Bradford and Harrogate, rest assured The Dales Way starts at Ilkley, (now in West Yorkshire since the 1974 boundary changes) and travels to Bowness, (now part of Cumbria).

So what exactly makes The Dales Way stand proud in comparison to other great walks? Without doubt, the greatest attribute it possesses is that it offers walkers of all ages, fitness and experience the opportunity to gain access to some of the most beautiful countryside this country has to offer. For the novice walker it provides an unparalleled introduction to long distance walking, with easy terrain and little demand on map work, whilst the more experienced walker will marvel at the contrast of this route in comparison with the more rugged and demanding walks of the Coast to Coast or Pennine Way.

The route provides a sprinkling of villages unspoilt throughout the centuries, having excellent accommodation, food and ale, together

1

with a living walk through history, from the early Roman occupation, the war torn middle ages, the Victorian Mills so commonly associated with the North, to the so called 20th century 'progression'. With all this to offer The Dales Way still has what I regard as its crowning glory, the people. Wherever you are on the route you will be made welcome, and it is to those people I say thank you for making this walk, "Seven glorious days."

The book has been designed to give every piece of information relevant to the walk, from basic planning, equipment and safety, to a comprehensive route description with strip maps, facilities and a Dales Way accommodation listed guide.

For this walk I joined a middle-aged couple, Ken and Chris on their first ever multi-day walk. Their peaks and troughs provide a valuable insight into the problems and pleasures any walker is likely to meet.

Enjoy the walk.

The Dales Way is a once in a lifetime experience, and by taking your time and soaking in the surroundings you too could have -
SEVEN GLORIOUS DAYS.

The Old Post Office, Bolton Abbey.

SYMBOLS USED ON THE MAPS

_←--← Dales Way Route

←o←o←o← Diversionary Dales Way Route

River

Road

Railway Line

Track

② Special Interest Point, in conjunction with Points of Interest Sections

Church

Ⓥ Special Viewpoint

Bridge

Woodland

Other Buildings

4½ Miles from Ilkley

Camp Site

Wall

Outcrop

THE DALES WAY ASSOCIATION

The Dales Way is an ever increasingly popular walk and in 1991 The Dales Way Association, which is a totally voluntary institution was formed to give detailed information to the walker and to protect the countryside through which the route passes.

The work of the Association has, without doubt, contributed much to this superb walk, and becoming a member of the Association is something I would recommend to anyone contemplating the walk.

The aims of The Dales Way Association are, in their own words ....

- To consider the route and status of The Dales Way Long Distance Footpath and related footpath links, and to support their appropriate maintenance, signing and way marking.

- To encourage the interpretation and conservation of The Dales Way and the landscape corridor through which it passes.

- To take an active role in the marketing and promotion of The Dales Way in ways that help to retain its essential character.

- To keep an up to date register of accommodation, route changes, transport and related facilities for the benefit of users of The Dales Way.

For a meagre £4 per annum the walker joining The Dales Way Association not only receives up to the minute news in the form of a Handbook and twice yearly newsletters, but also knows that they are helping this body to preserve one of the premier walks in the country for the enjoyment of future generations.

the dales way ©

To join The Dales Way Association couldn't be simpler. Just send a cheque for £4 made payable to 'The Dales Way Association' to:

Mr David Smith
Honorary Secretary
The Dales Way Association
Dalegarth
Moorfield Road
Ilkley, West Yorkshire. LS29 8BL

PREPARING FOR A WALK

Through the years there have been countless occasions where walkers have put themselves and others into dangerous and unfortunately sometimes fatal situations because they were ill prepared for the task they were undertaking. Walking, just like any other sport or pastime can be dangerous if basic guidelines are not followed. The walker who ventures onto hills prepared for any eventuality will have a safe and enjoyable time.

Many years ago before venturing into The Duke of Edinburgh's Gold Award Expedition I was given the best advice I have ever had ...... ESP

EQUIPMENT .... SAFETY .... PLANNING

By remembering ESP the foundations for a safe and prosperous venture into long distance walking are laid, whether it be a low level Dales walk, or a more rugged mountaineering trek.

EQUIPMENT

The range of equipment carried is, of course, an individual choice, however, there are certain items of equipment that are essential to any trek. Some of these items may never be put to use, but should any emergency occur the walker is equipped and ready to deal with the situation.

In recent years the outdoor pursuits industry has made significant inroads into the development of quality, lightweight equipment. Whilst the top of the range is still taxing on most people's pocket, the middle ground is affordable and satisfactory to the needs of the average walker.

So, just what is needed to commence a walk? Before each and every walk I have a stringent checklist on what I am wearing and what I am carrying - essential and otherwise. As already stated choice is an individual preference. Only intended as a reference guide this is my personal checklist. The items marked (E) are regarded as essential.

WALKING ATTIRE

A good pair of *sturdy walking boots (E).* Should be well fitted giving good ankle support and with a good tread.

Pure *wool walking socks (E).* Plus undersocks that are not nylon, as this will make your feet hot and prone to blistering.

Walking Trousers (E). These should be as light as possible and comfortable. Jeans should be avoided as these tighten when wet and will restrict movement, as well as taking much longer than normal trousers to dry.

Underwear (E). They may not be everyones idea of fashion but in colder weather the Long Johns are still in a class of their own.

'T' Shirt and Sweatshirt. Once on the move body heat quickly rises and too much outer clothing will sap strength.

CONTENTS OF THE PACK

Rucksack (E). There are numerous rucksacks available. Choose one that is not only large enough but also comfortable. Ideally it should be equipped with padded shoulder straps and supportive waist strap. I find that a sixty litre sack is more than adequate for my needs. The inside of the rucksack should be lined with bin liners, the rain does tend to seep in, and if everything is protected in plastic then your equipment will remain dry. When packing a rucksack the heaviest items should be placed at the top, it will be much easier to carry.

Waterproofs (E). Good quality waterproofs will make the difference between enjoying a walk and being thoroughly miserable. Carrying both leggings and top will ensure the best possible protection and should be stored within easy reach.

Maps (E). Ordnance Survey maps of the walking area are needed. The 1:25000 Outdoor Leisure maps are ideal, or if unavailable, the 1:50000 Landranger Series are adequate. Map reading ability is important and if not proficient the walker should seek tuition.The local library should be able to provide details on where qualified instruction can be gained.

Compass (E). Another vital piece of equipment. Working in harmony with map reading, the ability to use a compass is essential.

Whistle and Torch (E). Vital safety items explained in the following section.

First Aid Kit, Water Bottle and Survival Bag (E). Even on a day walk it is essential to carry a first aid kit and survival bag. If travelling in a party at least two first aid kits should be carried within the team. Further details under safety.

Woollen Hat (E). Over 70% of all body heat is lost through the top of the skull.
Gloves (E). To ensure the extremities are kept warm.
Guide Book. Whilst the guide book is there to offer the benefit of a fellow walker's experience, pointing out the route and highlighting the particular points of interest, the walker ultimately relies on their own skill with a map and compass to successfully complete the venture.

Spare clothing and footwear. At the end of a good days walking there is no better feeling than arriving at your accommodation, and, after a hot bath having a full change of attire.

Here is the 'spares' list carried by yours truly .... underwear, 3 'T' shirts, sweatshirt, trousers or tracksuit bottoms, socks and a light pair of shoes or trainers.
Other items carried include toiletries, towel, pen, pencil, spare boot laces, spare batteries, spare whistle, food to last a minimum of 24 hours.
Once packed this sample rucksack will weigh no more than between 35 and 40 pounds, which is a fairly acceptable weight to be carrying on a long distance walk. If the intention is to backpack, ie camping along the route, then the weight of camping equipment will significantly increase the amount carried.

SAFETY

Having the equipment mentioned in the previous section is a giant step towards ensuring not only your own safety on the fells, but also the well being of others, whether in your party or a chance encounter.

Whilst walking is predominantly a safe pastime accidents do occur and in the areas where these accidents happen there is every likelihood that safety is a few miles away. It is imperative therefore, for the walker to take every possible precaution, to first reduce the chances of mishaps and secondly to know how to deal with them should they occur.

REDUCING THE RISK

The risk factor is always there, for a novice and veteran alike. However, by following a few simple guidelines the risks are greatly reduced. The greater the knowledge, the less the risk.

Walking alone creates the greatest risk, and whilst many walkers prefer to walk alone, yours truly included, it is far safer to walk as a member of a group.

By learning to be proficient in first aid, map reading and compass work confidence is achieved in the control of any situation. When a map or guide book refers to a 'footpath' the reality is often a barely visible, trampling of the earth, regularly crossing tree roots and boulders etc, and a sprain, or worse is always a distinct possibility. Knowing how to deal with the situation is essential. Courses on basic first aid are regularly conducted in most areas and by qualified bodies. A few classes during the long winter nights will reap huge benefits when out on the hills, not only personally, but also to the benefit of fellow walkers.

Prior to any walk the route for the day should be planned and logged with a responsible adult, giving as much information as possible, including expected time of arrival at the destination. Leaving the route with the proprietor of the previous nights accommodation is a good way of ensuring the authorities are kept informed in case of mishap. When arriving at the destination the person left with the route should be contacted and informed of a safe arrival. It is vital that this person is told in order not to waste the time of the emergency services. Once decided and logged STICK TO THE ROUTE, and should anything happen the rescue services know where to start looking.

WHAT TO DO IN CASE OF AN ACCIDENT

It is important to remain calm and assess the situation. Check the casualty and try to determine the extent of their injuries, it may be with a sprain that the victim can be helped to safety. If the patient cannot be moved or there is the slightest doubt about moving them, leave them exactly where they are and administer first aid if needed. Keep them warm and get them into the survival bag. Do not at this stage go charging off for help. First of all take a triangulation to determine your exact location. Make a note of the grid reference and hand it to the person(s) going for help, then check the map to see where the nearest point of help is. Beware that many buildings marked on OS maps are derelict, look especially for marked telephone boxes. Once decided on which route is the quickest to alert help write it down and leave it with the person remaining with the casualty. Do not give the casualty any approximation on when a rescue is likely to be made, if it takes longer than expected the morale of the patient will be severely reduced. Now is the time to set off for help, armed with the grid reference number of the casualty's location. The tendency is to run for help, but another accident will double the crisis, so a brisk walk is more sensible. Always leave a member of the party with the casualty, it can be vital to ensure they remain conscious.

Once reaching the nearest point of help dial 999 and ask for Mountain Rescue. The caller will then be connected with the nearest police station and they will coordinate the evacuation, remembering to give them the grid reference number and to follow their explicit instructions.

This is all very well with a group of walkers, but what about the pair or lone walker? If alone the decision as to whether to try and get to safety is your own. If unable to continue then keep warm by putting on extra clothing and climbing into the survival bag. Take the whistle and start echoing the distress signal, which is SIX blasts every minute. If dark, then give the same signal with both torch and whistle. If the route has been logged with someone as advised help will locate you, but be ready for a lengthy wait if necessary.

If walking with one person who gets injured, then a decision has to be made whether or not it would be safe to leave the casualty. If in doubt then remain with the injured party and start giving the distress signal.

By now you are probably thinking twice about taking up this dangerous leisure sport called walking, but reality is that walking is extremely safe when done properly. This section only covers what action should be taken if anything should go wrong. In more than thirty years of mountaineering and walking I have had just one minor injury.

PLANNING

Before attempting any long distance trek the walker must know his/her own limitations. The experienced walker will already know what sort of distance they are comfortable in covering each day, but for the novice it really is a trip into the unknown and much will depend on age and level of fitness before deciding what distances are acceptable. Experience in map work, compass work and getting into a routine of carrying a rucksack for more than one day is essential.

A multi-day walk is very different from a day walk. The limbs have a very short recovery time overnight and the constant pounding of boot on earth is draining. After a couple of weekend jaunts it is possible to decide the sort of distance the walker feels comfortable in achieving daily. This is a personal choice and care should be taken. There is little point in over estimating the daily mileage, that will only lead to misery. Know your limitations and stick to them.

Many years ago I used to aim for at least twenty miles a day and it took a long while for me to realise what I was missing. I was so concerned with pounding out the mileage and was oblivious to the whole concept of walking. When I learned my lesson the countryside became a new world, a world that could be enjoyed and teach me so much. Today I plan a walk and if possible averaging no more than ten to twelve miles daily. That way I have a gentle pace, time to observe, and time to visit all the places of interest along the route.

There are times however when the walker has to cover more than the normal daily average. Even on The Dales Way, the section of seventeen miles contains very little in the way of facilities or accommodation, and so be prepared to cover this length of the walk when required.

When planning any long distance walk the route should be broken down into comfortable daily sections, taking into account the terrain covered. If there is a lot of climbing involved then the mileage will be reduced. Facilities along the route for intended breaks and accommodation for the night all need to be considered.

THE DALES WAY

As a guide this is how I separated The Dales Way into daily sections. It is only a guideline and you may wish to take longer spending more time walking or exploring the villages, towns and countryside.

Day 1	*Ilkley to Appletreewick*	*11.75 miles*
Day 2	*Appletreewick to Kettlewell*	*12.25 miles*
Day 3	*Kettlewell to Hubberholme*	*5.5 miles*
Day 4	*Hubberholme to Lea Yeat*	*17.25 miles*
Day 5	*Lea Yeat to Sedbergh*	*10.25 miles*
Day 6	*Sedbergh to Grayrigg*	*12.00 miles*
Day 7	*Grayrigg to Bowness*	*16.00 miles*

As can be clearly seen there is mileage covered every day. Day 3 I regarded as a 'rest day' a chance to relax whilst still keeping the limbs working, preparing for the long trek the following day. Ken and Chris, the couple I accompanied for most of the walk decided to have a complete rest day in Sedbergh and later confessed that this was the biggest mistake they made. They found it extremely difficult to get back into a walking rhythm after a day off.

Planning the walk correctly to suit individual needs is important.

Wherever possible it is advisable to book well in advance. The Dales Way is becoming more and more popular every year and whilst there is a good choice of accommodation it is limited. In this book each section contains Dales Way Association listed accommodation in a particular area.

The amount of time taken to walk The Dales Way is a personal choice. It is not a race, but it is there to be enjoyed at your leisure.

Bowness
Staveley
Burneside
Grayrigg
Cumbria
Sedbergh
LAKE DISTRICT NATIONAL PARK
Dent
Dent Head
Lea Yeat
Cam Houses
Hubberholme
Buckden
Starbotton
Kettlewell
North
Yorkshire
Grassington
Linton
Burnsall
Barden
Appletreewick
Bridge
Bolton Priory
Addingham
Ilkley
West Yorkshire

ILKLEY

Standing in the shadow of the famous Ilkley Moor on the edge of the Yorkshire Dales National Park, the town of Ilkley provides the official start to The Dales Way.

The history of Ilkley can be traced back as far as 79AD when the Romans built the fort of Olicana, which is now the site of the Manor House. When the Romans finally abandoned Olicana in the 4th or 5th century they left behind a settlement which formed the nucleus of the Anglo Saxon village. Christianity is known to have been introduced to the Northern Anglo Saxons by St Paulinus in 627AD, and the Saxon crosses in the All Saints Parish Church provide evidence that a church has existed here since the 8th and 9th centuries.

Ilkley remained a village for many years and although the Old Grammar School was built in 1637 it was not until the middle of the 18th century that the story of Ilkley, the town, really starts, for it was then that two spa baths were created at White Wells. The icy cold waters of the mineral springs were thought to be the cure for many ailments and the popularity of these Hydro's gave rise to the town, so much so, that by the 1890's there were no fewer than fifteen Hydro's in and around Ilkley.

As the town grew it took a new look. The customary shops appeared, a walk along Brook Street providing a glimpse at some of the oldest surviving shops, whilst The Grove gives an insight into the splendour of the Victorian era.

By the end of the 19th century the popularity of the spring water cures had all but vanished and Ilkley became a more conventional holiday town and so to its credit still is today.

Before setting off on this walk I spent a full day exploring this fascinating town and enjoyed every minute of it. I hope you have time to do the same.

FACILITIES

Eating   Ilkley provides a comprehensive supply of English, Chinese and Indian Restaurants together with Take-Aways.

Pubs   More than enough Ale Houses to satisfy even the thirstiest of walkers, the majority offering the option of real ale. Meals are available at most of the pubs. I tried a lunchtime meal at the Rose and Crown and found both the food and service second to none. In the evening I took solace at the Ilkley Moor Vaults with its church pews and bare floor boarded lounge, where conversation is not interrupted by Juke Box or television..

Shops   An excellent array of outlets for any last minute purchases you may have to make.

Accommodation as listed by The Dales Way Association.
The Grove Hotel, 66 The Grove, LS29 9PA. Tel: 01943 600298.
Mrs Terry, Belvedere, 2 Victoria Av., LS29 0ET.Tel: 01943 607598.
Mrs Below, Archway Cottage, 24 Skipton Road, LS29 9EP. Tel: 01943 603399.
Moorview Hotel, 104 Skipton Road, LS29 9HE. Tel: 01943 600156.
Mrs Read, 126 Skipton Road, LS29 9BQ. Tel: 01943 600635.
Mrs Roberts, 63 Skipton Road, LS29 9HF. Tel: 01943 817542.
Hollygarth Guest House, 293 Leeds Road, LS29 8LL. Tel: 01943 609223.
Mrs Kingdon, Wards End, Langbar, LS29 0ET. Tel: 01943 601577.

The Old Bridge, Ilkley.

ILKLEY TO ADDINGHAM
2.5 miles   EASY

On leaving the Railway Station turn right and right again down New Brook Street. At the traffic lights continue ahead with All Saints Church on the left. Immediately before the bridge turn left onto a public footpath leading through the riverside gardens to **The Old Bridge (1).** The sign **'The Dales Way, Bowness 73 miles' (2)** marks the official start of the walk.

The first few paces along the route are through a tree enclosed pathway with the splendid River Wharfe on the right. Soon the road leading to the Lawn Tennis and Squash Club is joined and curving to the right until level with the entrance where a footpath leads off to the left. Follow this path through open countryside and although not well defined a series of kissing gates helps the walker keep on course. The path leads through trees and rejoins the river for a short distance before meeting the old road towards Addingham.

Follow the road until a junction on the right leads towards the idyllic hamlet of Low Mill. Continue to follow the road between the houses to a gravelled cul-de-sac and from here take the footpath leading into **Addingham (4).**

When level with **St Peter's Church (3)** on the right, follow the footpath down towards the church, passing the building on the low side across open ground and to a small bridge on the left.

From here the actual route crosses a footbridge to the right between a cluster of cottages and bears right up North Street. However a small detour will lead into the heart of this busy yet pleasant village.

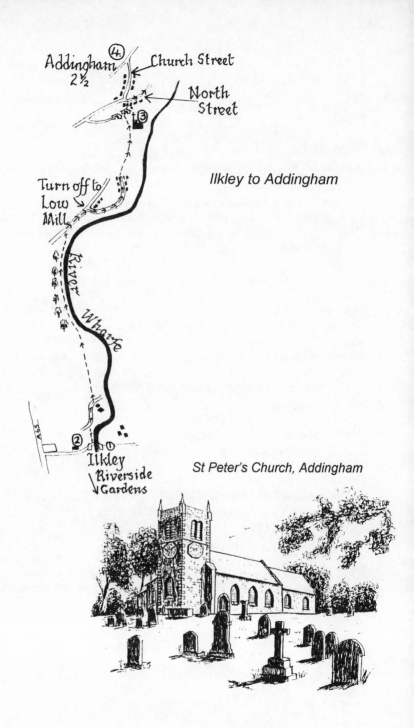

Addingham
2½
④ ← Church Street
North Street ←

③

Ilkley to Addingham

Turn off to
Low
Mill →

River Wharfe

A65

②

①

Ilkley
Riverside
Gardens

St Peter's Church, Addingham

POINTS OF INTEREST

The Old Packhorse Bridge (1), was erected in 1675 and is close to the site of the ford which the Roman Road originally used as it crossed the River Wharfe. The markings on the bridge denote the levels reached by the river when in flood.

The Dales Way Sign, Ilkley (2) although stating 73 miles the walk is actually 85 miles.

St Peter's Church, Addingham (3) was built during the 18th century and on an ancient site. Archbishop Wulfere took sanctuary here in 867 and a reminder of this period in history is the stone Saxon cross. The nave roof and chancel date from the 15th century. Plaques in the church commemorate the Cunliffe Lister family.

Addingham Village (4). To enter the village leave the route as you pass between the houses leading into North Street and cross the road into Church Street, by bearing slightly right at the end of the road, access to Addingham is gained.

FACILITIES

Addingham has a selection of pubs offering lunches and evening meals. There is also a fish and chip shop, coffee shop, Post Office and stores.

ACCOMMODATION

Mrs B Goodwin, 27 Wharfe Park, LS29 0QZ. Tel: 01943 831370.
Olicana Cottage, High Mill Lane, LS29 0RD. Tel 01943 830500. This cottage is at High Mill on the Dales Way.
Mr Proctor, 3 Bradley Rise, Silsden, BD20 9LZ Tel 01535 655887. 3 miles SW of the route. Transport to and from the route is available upon request.

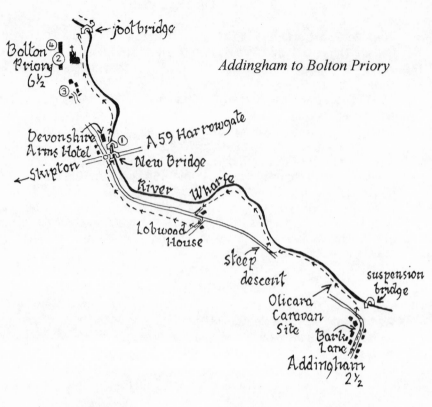

foot bridge

Bolton Priory 6½

Addingham to Bolton Priory

Devonshire Arms Hotel

A59 Harrowgate

←Skipton

New Bridge

River Wharfe

Lobwood House

steep descent

suspension bridge

Olicana Caravan Site

Bark Lane

Addingham 2½

Bolton Bridge

18

ADDINGHAM TO BOLTON PRIORY
4 miles   EASY

Leave Addingham via North Street. Climb the hill which merges into Bark Lane. After the road sweeps left take the footpath on the right which leads back to the river and a small suspension bridge. Ignore this bridge and continue along the path upstream, and with the River Wharfe still on your right. The well defined footpath leads to the main entrance to Olicana Caravan Site. Enter the site continuing two hundred yards until meeting a footpath to your right which returns to the riverbank, where the route gently meanders adjacent to the river. Follow the signs which occasionally deviate from the river.

When the river makes a sharp detour to the left the route leads into the trees and joins the road as it passes the house on the left. Turn left and then right into the entrance to Lobwood House. Cross the stone stile to the right and follow the way, parallel with the road, ignoring the ensuing wooden stile which leads back to the road. Cross the footbridge and on reaching the gate at the end of the field, a stile on the right leads to the road. Cross carefully and follow the footpath to **Bolton Bridge (1).**

From the bridge the path continues uninterrupted through the beautiful landscaped grounds to the incredible **Bolton Priory (2).**

On the approach to the Priory the accompanying hamlet of **Bolton Abbey (3)** is off to the left. Go up the steps and emerging through an archway in the surrounding wall is the village. Once through the archway an about turn will give a view of the Priory that has inspired many famous artists and poets, whilst to the left is the magnificent **Bolton Hall (4).**

POINTS OF INTEREST

Bolton Bridge (1): Until the opening of the A59 bypass in the 1990's this imposing structure bore the main through traffic from Skipton to Harrogate. It is also a significant entry point into the Yorkshire Dales National Park.

Bolton Priory (2): This splendid relic of English history is covered in detail on the following pages.

Bolton Abbey (3): Whilst the Priory is often referred to as the Abbey, Bolton Abbey is in fact the accompanying hamlet. The splendid Post Office and coffee Shop provide a picture postcard scene. The Post Office is soon to be relocated beside the very busy car park.

Bolton Hall (4): The tower, the centre point of the building was originally the Gatehouse to the Priory. The Hall is now used as a Hunting Lodge by the Duke of Devonshire.

FACILITIES

Bolton Bridge offers a cafe (check opening times), one pub and a Public Telephone.
Bolton Abbey has a quaint coffee shop, Post Office/gift shop, public telephone and toilets.

ACCOMMODATION

None

BOLTON PRIORY

In 1120 an order of Augustinian Canons was founded at Embsay near Skipton, but the volatile nature of the times led them to seek safety elsewhere.

In 1154 the black robed canons came across the hills from Embsay to start a more secure life afforded them by the Lady Alice De Romille of Skipton Castle. Whilst predominantly occupied by prayer, worshipping seven times a day, the canons, often local men, lived a monastic but not reclusive life, harmonising into the community by teaching, giving medical care and aiding travellers through the region, as well as acting as parish priests, allowing full access to their priory.

The money needed to build their magnificent Priory was raised by growing their own produce, collecting rents from tithes, local farms, mills and lead mines which had been either given to them or purchased. A tithe barn was used by anyone needing storage. One tenth of the income from the produce stored in the barn would be paid to the monks as rent.

Unfortunately work was constantly interrupted by either a lack of funds or the skirmishes against the marauding Scots, and it was not until 1520 that work finally started on the West Tower. Then in 1539 after King Henry VIII had severed all links with Rome and the Catholic Church he ordered the obliteration of all monasteries. Work on the tower was immediately abandoned, the lead was stripped from the roof, the furnishings were ripped out and the land sold to the Clifford family and later became the property of the Cavendishes, Dukes of Devonshire.

Although the majority of this magnificent building was destroyed or abandoned the nave survived thanks to the efforts of Prior Moone, who made provision for the nave to be saved as a church for the local parishioners, under the wing of the newly formed Church of England.

On entering what is now the Parish Church, the facing wall (east) was erected in 1539 to separate the nave when the rest of the Priory was abandoned. It was rebuilt in 1877 and the wall painting, with five Madonna lilies representing the Virgin Mary and the other plants depicting various events in the life of Christ, completed three years later by Thomas Bottomley.

The Stone Altar is a rare example of a Pre-Reformation altar and was probably used by canons. The large recess once housed the brass plate now mounted on the wall.

It was not until the Gothic revival that the Priory started receiving the attention it so richly deserved and began to recapture a little of its former glory. Pugin, a leading light in the revival designed the stained glass window in 1853 and then in 1867 leading architect George Street was placed in charge of the restoration work which is still clearly visible today.

The window in the side aisle depicts St Cuthbert, a Saint more associated with Lindisfarne, an island off the North East coast of Northumberland. St Cuthbert is seen here as the Bishop of Lindisfarne carrying the head of St Oswald.

It is worth while exploring the rest of the nave and leaving time to admire the breathtaking atmosphere of this popular historic gem.

Further guide notes are available in the Priory.

As a walker I found the prayer in the 'welcome' guide very appropriate:

God be with you in your going out and your coming in,
God be with you in your work and in your leisure,
God be with you in life's hills and in its valleys,
God be with you in company and in solitude,
God be with you in your pilgrimage and at its end,
And the blessing of God the Father, Son and Holy Spirit abide with you always.
Amen.
(reproduced with kind permission of the Church of St Mary and St Cuthbert, Bolton Priory)

BOLTON PRIORY TO BARDEN BRIDGE
3 miles   EASY

Leaving Bolton Priory the walker has the first views of the river from the other bank. Cross the wooden footbridge and after bearing to the left take the clearly marked path up the hill. Whilst the climb is moderately steep, but short, the final view of Bolton Priory from the summit is well worth the climb.

The path now heads off down through the trees and as this is a popular walk with day trippers the pathway is clear but prone to diversions as certain ways are eroded. Cross Pickles Beck which runs over the footpath, by either forging straight ahead, or, if flooded by using the footbridge ten yards to the right. On leaving the woodland the route

Barden Bridge 9½

The stile marks the end of the strid.

③

The strid

follows alongside the river until meeting the bridge which returns the walker to the other bank of the river at **The Cavendish Pavillion (1).**

②

wooden bridge

①

ford

Once over the bridge the path leads into **The Strid Wood Nature Trail (2).** Follow the green trail which eventually exits at a stile and onto a further well defined footpath which then crosses the **aqueduct (3).** Turn immediately left and the route follows directly to Barden Bridge. Once there the route does not officially cross the bridge, however a small detour over this sturdy structure and following the road around to the left will lead to the remains of **Barden Tower (4).**

River Wharfe

⊘ Look back to Bolton Priory

wooden footbridge

Bolton Priory 6½

POINTS OF INTEREST

The Cavendish Pavillion (1). The expansion of the national railway networks in the 1800's allowed previously unavailable access to the countryside for thousands of urban dwellers. The Pavillion was built in 1880 as a tea room for these visitors.

The Strid Wood Nature Trail (2). A network of colour coded paths designed in the 19th century by the Reverend William Carr and providing an unparalleled display of fauna and flora.

There are five walks through the wood ranging from the more difficult red trail to the short low level amble along the yellow one. The 'strid' itself is the point in the river where the Wharfe is compressed between the rocks resulting in a narrow but gushing torrent. The word 'strid' derives from the river being a stride in width at this point, however it is not recommended that you try to cross the strid. Many people have come to grief in such a pursuit, alas, some fatally.

The Aqueduct (3): Built to carry water from Nidderdale to the busy conurbation of Bradford. You can hear the water gushing through the pipes beneath your feet as you cross.

Barden Tower (4): Barden was part of the Craven estates granted to Baron Robert De Romille after the Norman Conquest. The word 'Barden' means 'valley of the boar', and appropriately the tower was first used as a hunting lodge. It was during the Wars of the Roses that Henry, 10th Lord Gifford, whose father was a sworn enemy of the Yorkist King, hid at Barden posing as a shepherd. When in 1485

Barden Tower

24

Henry VII claimed the throne for the House of Lancaster the 'Shepherd Lord' as he became known remained at Barden instead of returning to Skipton Castle and greatly enlarged the tower and built the chapel. In 1513 Lord Clifford led his troops into the famous battle of Flodden Field and although surviving this bloody encounter died ten years later at the age of 70.

The tower fell into ruin until in 1643 Lady Anne Clifford inherited the land. Whilst Civil War prevented her from immediately beginning restoration, work did commence in 1657. As a memorial to the work carried out a plaque was inscribed and can be seen on the walls today.

From her death in 1676 Barden has not been lived in and was passed down to the Earls of Cork and Burlington and ultimately to the Duke of Devonshire.

FACILITIES

Cavendish Pavillion: Restaurant, tea, coffee, sandwiches. Public telephone, toilets and gift shop.

Barden Tower: Licensed restaurant, tea, coffee, sandwiches and toilets.

ACCOMMODATION

Howgill: Howgill Lodge, Barden, Skipton, North Yorkshire. BD23 6DJ. Tel: 01756 720655. B & B and camp site.

BARDEN BRIDGE TO BURNSALL
4.25 miles   EASY

Leave Barden Bridge on the same side of the river as the approach and keeping the river on your left. Follow the road for approximately 50 yards before a walled stile on the left leads onto a distinct footpath. This path leads alongside the river and is a very easy and comfortable stroll. It was alongside this stretch I first encountered Ken and Chris whose comments appear from here onwards.

The route continues for 1.75 miles before, approaching Howgill the path is forced away from the river bank. Veer to the right and the path joins the road, and, keeping to the left cross the road bridge. The path to the left returns to the river bank and the footpath continues to **Appletreewick (1).**

After almost a mile from Howgill a track to the right leads up to **The New Inn (2),** and **The Craven Arms (3),** in the idyllic village of the unusually named Appletreewick. Whilst the actual Dales Way does not turn off at this point, continuing upstream towards Burnsall - it is well worth a short detour to visit this 'picture postcard' village. The track leading up to the New Inn is a private road and although access is allowed, there is a collection box at the top gate and a few coppers will ensure the upkeep of the access.

On rejoining the route follow the riverside footpath until the path is forced away from the river for a short time at Woodhouse Farm. Crossing the yard negotiate the footbridge through to the next gate. The footpath is distinct and returns to the river. The village of Burnsall can be seen ahead. Passing the public toilets in the field a left turn onto the road and across the bridge will lead directly into Burnsall.

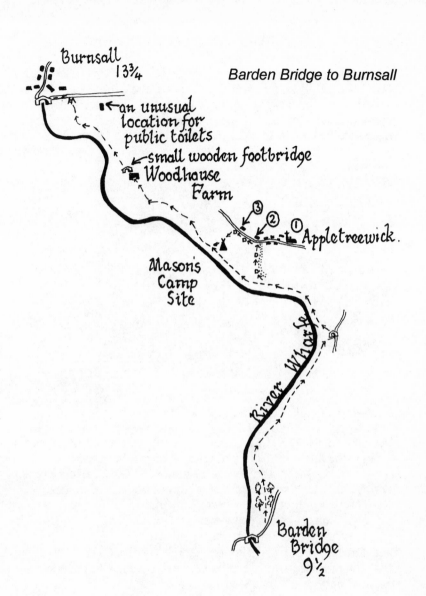

Burnsall
13¾

Barden Bridge to Burnsall

←an unusual
location for
public toilets

←small wooden footbridge

Woodhouse
Farm

③ ② ① Appletreewick.

Mason's
Camp
Site

River Wharfe

Barden
Bridge
9½

POINTS OF INTEREST

Appletreewick (1): The splendour of this village, pronounced Aptrick), is a joy to behold and a visit is a must even if not staying the night there. The history of the village can be traced back to the Norman Conquest and is actually in the Domesday Book.

The sketch below is of Mock Beggar Hall in the heart of the village. Built in 1697 this was originally the site of a Grange used many years previously by the monks from Bolton Priory.

Mock Beggar Hall, Appletreewick.

The other building of note is the tiny St Johns Church which contains furniture by 'Mousey' Thompson, famous for the unusual method of carving a mouse on each piece of furniture crafted. Every craftsman working for Thompson had his own individually carved mouse.

The New Inn (2): Clearly visible from the route, this welcome sight provides superb ale and conversation. The landlord is a veritable feast of information on walking and mountain biking.

The Craven Arms (3): Named after William Craven, who, born in 1548 left the village and became Lord Mayor of London. Later in life he returned and founded a school.

FACILITIES

Appletreewick: Two pubs both serving excellent beers. The New Inn provides meals at lunchtimes, The Craven Arms both lunchtime and evening. Public telephone.

Burnsall: Pub, post office, shop and public telephone.

ACCOMMODATION

Appletreewick
Masons Camp Site, Ainhams House, Appletreewick, Nr Skipton. BD23 6DD. Tel: 01756 720275. An excellent site.
Mr C A Knowles-Fitton, Knowles Lodge, Appletreewick, Skipton. BD23 6DQ. Tel: 01756 720228. (At Howgill).
Ms A M Coney, Blundellstead, Appletreewick, Skipton. BD23 6DB. Tel: 01756 720632.
Mrs Jackson, Andra's Farm, Appletreewick, Skipton. BD23 6DA. Tel: 01756 720286.
Mr J D Pitchers, The New Inn, Appletreewick, Skipton. BD23 6DA. Tel: 01756 720252.

The New Inn, Appletreewick.

Burnsall
Mrs C M Fitton, Valley View Guest House, Burnsall, Skipton. BD23 6BN. Tel: 01756 720314.
Mrs A Hall, Holly Tree Farm, Thorpe, Skipton. BD23 6BJ. Tel: 01756 720604. Pick up from Burnsall or Grassington if required. Transport for evening meal by arrangement.
Mrs A Mason, Conistone House, Burnsall, Skipton. BD23 6BN. Tel: 01756 720650.

BURNSALL TO GRASSINGTON
3.5 miles MODERATE

Leave Burnsall having crossed the road bridge towards the village. Bear immediately right next to the Red Lion Hotel and back onto the riverside footpath. The way is clearly defined and is a pleasant walk past the Loup Scar and on towards the **suspension footbridge (1)**.

Cross the bridge, turn left and continue along a pleasant riverside walk for another mile, before temporarily leaving the Wharfe and heading across the field. Cross the small bridge about half way across the field. On the left is the sewerage works whilst The Dales Way gradually bears to the right past a fish farm and onto a well defined track. Take note of the sign on the first gate, the actual footpath enters the field again another 50 yards further on. The footpath at this point is fairly clear and with **Linton Church (2)** to the left on the opposite bank, leads to the Bridge at **Linton Falls (3).** Do not cross the bridge, the route carries straight on with the river remaining on the left.

Gradually the path veers away from the river and passes below a row of cottages before emerging at the bridge at **Grassington (4)**. Once onto the road bear right up the steep incline and this will bring you into the heart of this busy little 'town'.

17¼

Grassington

Threshfield   cottages   Sedbergh Lane

gate

Fish Farm

stile

footbridge

N

Sewage works

River Wharfe

Suspension footbridge (Beware)

Loup Scar

Burnsall 13¾

30

POINTS OF INTEREST

The Suspension Bridge (1). It's definitely 'heart in the mouth time' as this is crossed. The bridge tends to travel downstream as you cross it and as if this wasn't enough it is extremely narrow and difficult to negotiate laden with a rucksack.

Linton Church (2). Although off route a visit to this shrine of medieval architecture is a must. Built well away from the village it probably replaced an ancient pagan shrine.

Linton Falls (3). An ideal place for a break, especially if you do not want the hustle and bustle of Grassington. In recent years the water level of the River Wharfe, like most Yorkshire rivers has been in decline, however, if the river is in full flow this is a truly memorable resting place.

Linton Falls

Grassington (4). Excepting Ilkley and Bowness Grassington is certainly the busiest place en-route, yet still retaining its undoubted charm and character. Extremely popular with touring coach parties.

FACILITIES

Grassington: As one would expect this town offers a full range of facilities, including good pubs, numerous coffee shops, gift shops and a fish and chip shop.

ACCOMMODATION

Linton

The Youth Hostel, Linton In Craven, Skipton. BD23 5HH. Tel 01756 752 400. This hostel is not open all the year round.

Grassington

Grassington

Mrs Berry, Springroyd House, 8a Station Road, Grassington, Skipton. BD23 5NQ. Tel: 01756 752473.

Mr A Colley, Lythe End, Wood Lane, Grassington, Skipton. BD23 5DF. Tel: 01756 753196.

Mrs Cullingford, Craven Cottage Restaurant, Main Street, Grassington, Skipton. BD23 5AA. Tel 01756 752205.

Mr & Mrs Elsworth, Grassington House Hotel, Grassington, Skipton. BD23 5AQ. Tel 01756 752406.

Mr & Mrs Lingard, The Lodge Guest House, 8 Wood Lane, Grassington, Skipton. BD23 5LU. Tel 01756 752518.

Mrs M Lister, Town Head Guest House, 1 Low Lane, Grassington, Skipton. BD23 5AU. Tel 01756 752811.

Mr & Mrs Lockyer, Kirkfield, Hebden Road, Grassington, Skipton. BD23 5LJ. Tel 01756 752385.

Mr & Mrs Marsden, Burtree Cottage, Hebden Road, Grassington, Skipton. BD23 5LH. Tel 01756 752442.

Mrs Richardson, The Foresters Arms, Main Street, Grassington, Skipton. BD23 5AA. Tel 01756 752349.

Mrs S Trewartha, Mayfield, Old Mill Lane, Grassington, Skipton. BD23 5BX. Tel 01756 753052.

Mr & Mrs Whitfield, 47 Main Street, Grassington, Skipton. BD23 5BB. Tel 01756 752069.

Mrs E Thompson, Wood Nook, Skirethorns, Threshfield, Skipton. BD23 5NU. Tel 01756 752412. (Camp site only).

GRASSINGTON TO CONISTONE PIE
3.75 miles   MODERATE

Leave Grassington by continuing up the main street until meeting Chapel Street on the left. Continue along Chapel Street for a few hundred yards before meeting the entrance to the farm on the right where the road bends sharply to the left. Enter the farmyard and follow the way markers which lead to the left, and on reaching the gate access is gained to the open countryside. Follow the path along the side of the wall and on reaching the end of the track begin to bear very gradually left through two stiles before emerging into **Lea Green (1)**.

At this point the path is slightly indistinct and great care should be taken. On reaching the much wider track cross straight over it and continue upwards leading onto a windswept walk across the top, ignoring another trampled footway to the left.

Ahead can be seen a rocky knoll and by keeping this slightly to the left the correct route will be followed and eventually bearing right to cross two stiles before skirting the knoll. At this point the way is fairly clear and rises gently to the lime kiln on the left - a haven if walking in windy conditions.

On leaving the kiln, the route is easy and straight forward until reaching Conistone Dib, where confusion can occur. Ignore the stile and keeping to the right cross the much wider track which leads to a clear walk through to the impressive **Conistone Pie (2).** Whilst the route includes this magnificent wonder of nature on the walkers left, a small detour to the summit provides an outstanding view of the fells and the valleys below.

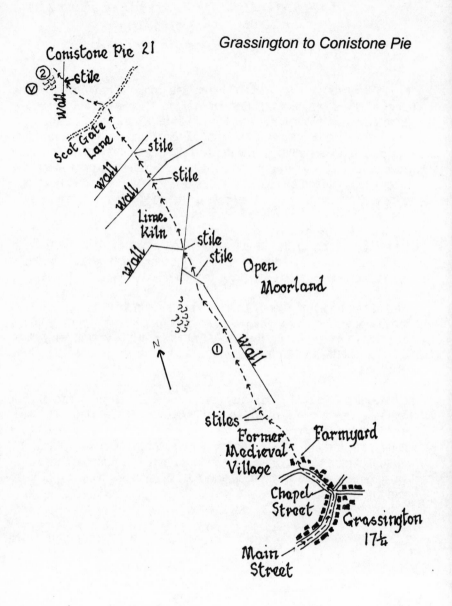

Conistone Pie 21

② ←stile

Ⓥ Wall

Scot Gate Lane

Wall ← stile

Wall ← stile

Lime Kiln

Wall ← stile

stile

Open Moorland

N

① Wall

stiles

Former Medieval Village

Farmyard

Chapel Street

Grassington 17½

Main Street

POINTS OF INTEREST

Lea Green (1). The remains of an ancient settlement and field system.
Conistone Pie (2). On the approach to this incredible wonder the unknowing, would, without doubt, believe this to be a man-made edifice, however, the limestone work of nature is totally natural and provides one of the premier views of the whole walk. The panoramic sketch identifies the major constuctions.

View from Conistone Pie

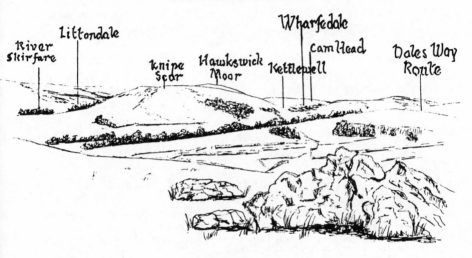

FACILITIES

None between Grassington and Conistone Pie, however, by collecting supplies in Grassington Conistone Pie provides an unequalled location for a packed lunch.

ACCOMMODATION

None after Grassington. Next available accommodation is in Kettlewell.

CONISTONE PIE TO KETTLEWELL
3.35 miles EASY

To leave such a breathtaking view is never easy, but alas the route must continue. Descend from the Pie and rejoin the distinct track. The walk is easy, interrupted by the occasional stile, until meeting a gate in the corner of a copse. Pass through the gate and the path leads steeply downhill, past Scargill House on the right until meeting the old road. Bear right and after a few hundred yards the actual route bears off to the right onto a footpath leading to the eastern extremity of **Kettlewell (1)**. This path leads over several stiles and can be quite boggy in wetter conditions. If following this route, when reaching the road at the last of the stiles turn left and walk into the village. On reaching the junction by the Kings Head turn right and then first left to gain access to the shops and two other pubs.

Alternatively, if weariness and bad weather are prevalent the easier route into Kettlewell is to follow the road all the way.

Novice walkers should note that this stretch provides the first encounter with open moorland. Ken and Chris found that although the walk over Conistone was exhilarating for the views, the terrain also provided testament as to why an intimate knowledge of map and compass is essential.

Kettlewell 2¼

See narrative

Numerous stiles and gates

Easier Diversion Route

Scargill House

steep descent
Highgate Leys Lane

Road to Conistone

wall
stile

wall
stile

N

stile   wall
stile   wall

Conistone Pie 21

POINTS OF INTEREST

Kettlewell (1). The sort of village that every visitor to these shores imagines England to be - cottages of unrivalled character, three excellent traditional pubs and of course St Mary's Church, a 19th century building occupying a 12th century site. An overnight stay in Kettlewell is something to be enjoyed.

FACILITIES

Shops, public telephone, The Blue Bell Hotel, The Racehorses Hotel and The Kings Head - all three providing superb hosts, excellent meals and boast a splendid choice of Real Ale.

ACCOMMODATION

Campers please note: Whilst there is a campsite at the eastern end of the village it is extremely basic with only a portaloo on the actual site. If you require a shower or even warm water you have a lengthy walk back to the farmhouse in the village. Perhaps not what you need after walking all day.

Mrs J Elliott, Langcliffe House, Kettlewell, Skipton. BD23 5RJ. Tel: 01756 760243.
Mrs L Thornborrow, Lynburn, Langcliffe Garth, Kettlewell, Skipton. BD23 5RF. Tel: 01756 760803.
Mrs Morgan, Park Bottom, Litton, Skipton. BD23 5QJ. Tel: 01756 770235. (Situated within 50 yards of the Queens Arms, Litton. Transport can be provided, if required, to and from The Dales Way route).

KETTLEWELL TO HUBBERHOLME
5.5 miles   EASY

Leave Kettlewell by crossing the bridge by The Racehorses Hotel and bear right to the public footpath leading to the riverside. With the River Wharfe always in close proximity the way is clearly visible and leads through a number of gates and stiles for almost two miles, before reaching the bridge leading to Starbotton.

The more adventurous walker may wish to visit this sleepy hamlet standing in the shadows of Buckden Pike and Starbotton boasts the Fox and Hounds pub - a handy stop for the weary walker.

River Wharfe at Hubberholme.

To continue **do not cross the bridge** but follow the clearly defined path. Soon the river slopes off to the right, however, the path continues straight ahead until, as the river seems to meander its way back towards the route a wide track is joined. Passing the barn rejoin the river by means of a gate in the wall to the right.

Once back by the riverside an easy amble leads to Buckden Bridge and again, although the official route does not actually go to **Buckden (1),** a visit to this village is a pleasant and rewarding experience. Bear right from the bridge and this will lead you to the village.

On leaving Buckden Bridge cross the road and rejoin the public footpath almost directly opposite. Stay along the river bank until joining the road which leads to the amazing hamlet of **Hubberholme (2).**

Hubberholme
② 29¾

Kettlewell to Hubberholme

Dubbs Lane

① Buckden

Birks Wood

Firth Wood

River Wharfe

Starbotton

Diversion into Starbotton

St Michael and All Angels Church, Hubberholme.

Kettlewell 24¼

POINT OF INTEREST

Buckden (1). The history of Buckden can be traced back as far as medieval times when the village was used as a base for the massive hunting grounds surrounding it. A pleasant village, well worth a visit.
Hubberholme (2). A magnificent hamlet with an expanded history on the following pages.

FACILITIES

Buckden: village store, public telephone, post office and public toilets. The Buck Inn, also in the village, by its name shows links with the village's hunting history.
Hubberholme: The George Inn.

ACCOMMODATION

Mr K Horsman, Whimsical Cottage, Buckden, Nr Skipton. BD23 5JA. Tel: 01756 760827.
Mr & Mrs Lightfoot, Ghyll Cottage, Buckden, Nr Skipton. BD23 5JA. Tel: 01756 760399.
Miss Thornborrow, West Winds, Buckden, Nr Skipton. BD23 5JA. Tel: 01756 760883.
Mrs Tupling, Romany Cottage, Buckden, Nr Skipton. BD23 5JA. Tel: 01756 760365.
Mrs Falshaw, The Grange Farm, Hubberholme, Nr Skipton. BD23 5JE. Tel: 01756 760259. (Bunk barn accommodation).
Mrs Huck, Church Farm, Hubberholme, Nr Skipton. BD23 5JE. Tel: 01756 760240.
The George Inn, Hubberholme, Nr Skipton. BD23 5JE. Tel: 01756 760223.

HUBBERHOLME
(pronounced Hubber-rum)

Nestling beneath the imposing fells of Langstrothdale and sitting on the banks of the River Wharfe the Idyllic hamlet of Hubberholme takes its name from the invading Viking King with the unfortunate name of 'HubbaThe Berserker'.

This sparse sprinkling of humanity still surviving from the Norse invasions boast two places of immense interest, which, when you consider the whole hamlet consists of maybe half a dozen buildings is a considerable achievement.

St Michael and All Angels Church is a really remarkable sight. The church was originally constructed in the 13th century and includes an oak 'rood' loft, one of only two remaining in the whole of Yorkshire, the other being at Flamborough.

The 'rood loft' is the archway separating the chancel from the nave and was originally a balcony often used by the minister to conduct the service. The rood is the crucifix standing on the balcony and was installed in St Michael's in 1558.

Many years ago the landlord of the nearby George Inn would also be the Parish Clerk and the altar in the chancel was used as the Inn's Ale Bench!! Wherever you look in this historical gem you are surrounded by amazing sights. Pews manufactured by 'Mousey' Thompson with the carved mouse on the side, the 'Prayer Tree' - a more modern development on which prayers are written on paper and left on the tree, for the congregation to use and incorporate into the next service.

Just prior to my visit BBC Television had been using the church as a location for the drama, 'The Tenant of Wildfell Hall'.
Like most churches all along the route St Michael's is not only of historical interest but still provides a service to the local community.

A visit here is a must and normally the church is open from 9.00 a.m. until dusk. Stop, visit and explore.

The author J B Priestley loved this quiet hamlet and was a frequent visitor and it is fitting that when he died his ashes were scattered in the grounds of the church.

From the church it is a short hop across the bridge to discover one of the most pleasant pubs that I have visited. The George Inn, full of 18th century character and charm. On entering you cannot help being impressed by the magnificent open fire beneath a cast iron shroud, the very low beamed ceiling or the bare flagstone floor. The George has everything when it comes to 'ye good olde country pub'.

It is very rare that an establishment cannot be faulted, but on this occasion I have to say the ale, meals, hospitality and accommodation were excellent.

Throughout history The George and St Michael's have been closely linked and even now the traditional 'Hubberholme Parliament' is still held on the first Monday after the New Year. This is a ceremony in which the bar becomes a court with the local vicar presiding over the auctioning of the grazing rights to a 16 acre paddock.

Before leaving The George Inn enquire of the landlord the meaning of the ever burning candle placed at the bar.

The George Inn, Hubberholme.

If wallowing in the peaceful haven of Hubberholme was a pleasing experience then the next seventeen and a half miles prove to be a veritable feast of tranquillity, for the ensuing miles provide walking that, at least, can be best described as lonely, and as this section is walked in one day it is important that food stocks are replenished before setting out. With the welcome exception of Cam Houses (8.5 miles from Hubberholme), there is a total lack of facilities.

Leave Hubberholme by crossing the bridge and take the clearly marked footpath behind the church. After passing the churchyard follow the path away from the wider track to return to the river bank. There are a number of stiles and gates as the next two miles to **Yockenthwaite (1)** is a pleasant riverside stroll.

On reaching the farm buildings the route passes on the right side and does not, as is easy to imagine, drop down to the bridge, but continues straight ahead until a gate is reached, which then leads back to the riverside. Follow the river passing Yockenthwaite Cairn Circle and at the next stile the path starts to veer away from the river, until at the top of the field a footbridge is crossed before encountering the access road to Deepdale. Turn down the hill to the bridge at the bottom. Cross over the bridge and the path then joins the western bank of the river.

Once again the route is exceptionally well defined, passing New House Farm building on its way to Beckermonds hamlet. Cross the footbridge leading into the Beckermonds access road.

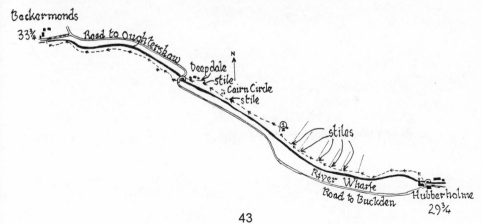

POINTS OF INTEREST

Yockenthwaite (1). The area around Yockenthwaite is littered with caves and potholes, so if you are a potholing fanatic who likes scrambling around in total darkness and up to your neck in water, then this is the area for you.

FACILITIES

None whatsoever. Please ensure that you are carrying sufficient supplies of food and drink to reach Lea Yeat.

Beckermonds

ACCOMMODATION

Mrs S Middleton, Low Raisgill Cottage, Yockenthwaite, Nr Hubberholme, Skipton BD23 5JQ. Tel; 01756 760351. Evening meal by arrangement, alternatively a taxi is provided to any local pub. Packed lunches are also available.

BECKERMONDS TO CAM HOUSES
4.5 miles MODERATE

Having reached the access road at Beckermonds the route then climbs fairly steeply to join the road. The expanse of grassland to the left appears to be a short cut, but it is not a footpath and therefore should not be used. At this point turn left and unfortunate as it may be, the next mile and a quarter takes the form of a road walk into Oughtershaw. Not until passing the final set of farm buildings on the left does the route regain a more comfortable texture, and as the road bends to the right join the wide track to the left.

Follow the track for what appears to be an eternity leading to Nethergill and finally Swarthgill. Upon reaching the house bear left through the gate and into open ground once more. If the weather is amiable the route, although not particularly well defined, can be seen well ahead. On the hill in the distance is **Cam Houses (1),** still almost a mile and a half away.

Continue along the footpath aiming for the derelict farm building ahead. This is Breadpiece Barn and as you reach it cross the first stile directly in front before turning sharply right to cross a second one. This then leads sharply up to Cam Houses and a welcome cuppa.

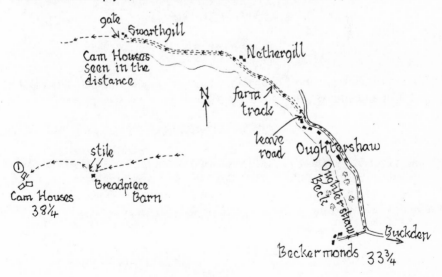

POINTS OF INTEREST

Cam Houses (1). On the long walk from Hubberholme to Lea Yeat Cam Houses provides the solitary access to food and drink. For many years Mr and Mrs Smith have provided the weary hiker with superb hospitality. On many occasions payment being accredited to the honesty of the hiker. Unfortunately over the past few years a minority of 'hikers' have not respected the value of Mr and Mrs Smith and as so often happens the thoughtless behaviour of a few mindless individuals threatens to spoil this crucial service. Appreciation and thanks to Mr and Mrs Smith who provide an unequalled service for The Dales Way explorer.

Approaching Cam Houses.

FACILITIES

Cam Houses provide the only form of sustenance in this section. Hot drinks and snacks are normally available.

ACCOMMODATION

Mrs Dorothy Smith, Cam Houses, Upper Langstrothdale, Buckden, Nr Skipton. BD23 5JT. Tel: 0860 648045. Bed and breakfast. Evening meal can be provided. Bunk barn accommodation is also available.

CAM HOUSES TO FAR GEARSTONES
3.25 miles   MODERATE

Before leaving the sanctuary of Cam Houses please refer to special 'Point of Interest 1'.

Continue past the bunk barn and as the access road bears to the right, the route continues straight ahead to a gate. Follow the path diagonally across the field to a stile in the fence and next to the plantation. Cross the stile and climb the steep path alongside the trees - this track can be exceptionally muddy even in the driest of conditions. The cairn at the top soon comes into view. Head straight towards the cairn to meet the **Cam High Road (2).** This is the point where **The Pennine Way (3)** meets The Dales Way. On reaching the high road bear left and the wide track leads in almost a mile to a parting of the ways at Cam End. Along this section of the route all three of the **Yorkshire Three Peaks (4)** can be seen.

At this point it worth stopping to admire the Ribblehead Viaduct which carries the Settle to Carlisle Railway. (See page 49).

From Cam End The Dales Way forks to the right downhill to meet the bridge at Gayle Beck. Negotiate the stile which will lead onto the road between Hawes and Ingleton at Far Gearstones.

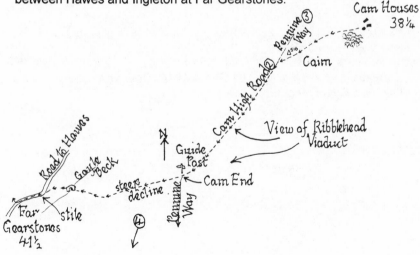

POINTS OF INTEREST

The Dales Way Route (1). The route from Cam Houses is liable to change as the original route has been illegally blocked by the forest plantation. This can lead to confusion and whilst the way is fairly clear, visible care should be taken not to stray from the route.
Cam High Road (2). The old Roman Road between their forts at Ingleton and Bainbridge in Wensleydale. Take care along this cobbled walk, a twisted ankle is easily attained.
The Pennine Way (3). At the cairn The Dales Way meets the oldest and most respected long distance walk in this country. Commencing in the 'picture postcard' village of Edale in the Derbyshire Peaks it travels more than 250 miles north to Kirk Yetholm on the Scottish borders. In the 20 years since I first walked the Pennine Way it has seen colossal changes. The route has been walked to death and whilst it is still rated as the number one long distance trek it really cannot stand in comparison with the beauty of The Dales Way.
The Yorkshire Three Peaks (4). A favourite test for hikers. The summits of Whernside, Ingleborough and Penyghent provide a stern examination of even the most experienced walker. A good days walking!

FACILITIES

None after leaving Cam Houses.

ACCOMMODATION

Mrs Doreen Timmins, Gearstones, Ribblehead, Ingleton, Carnforth, Lancashire. LA6 3AS. Tel: 015242 41405.
Mr Warwick, The Station Inn, Ribblehead, Ingleton, Carnforth, Lancashire. LA6 3AS. Tel: 015242 41274. Bed and breakfast and bunk barn accommodation.

ENGLAND'S MOST SCENIC RAILWAY
SETTLE TO CARLISLE

On the old Roman Road from Cam down to Gearstones the impressive Ribblehead Viaduct is seen in the far distance. For a few moments pause and contemplate the history of this awesome feat in British engineering.

Crossing The Ribblehead Viaduct.

The line actually opened in the August of 1875 but the story of the Settle to Carlisle begins seven years earlier. The Midland Railway were desperate for a new route leading directly from the industrial Midlands of England to Scotland and a young engineer C S Starland was dispatched to plot out the course of this new line. He certainly discovered the harshness of the Pennine winters, becoming snowbound for three weeks in the wayside inn that once adorned Gearstones.

The line runs for 72 miles and wherever possible follows the course of the River Ribble and then the River Eden to the outer reaches of Carlisle. Direct as it was the route would have to conquer some of the most difficult terrain imaginable for a railway. A dozen viaducts and five major tunnels - incredibly the longest at Blea Moor, one and a half miles long and carved through solid limestone and at times up to 500 feet below ground level - one of the greatest feats of engineering ever undertaken in this country.

Workers were drafted in from as far a field as Cornwall, Ireland and Scotland, arriving with their families. Disease ridden shanty towns sprang up wherever the line was under construction.

Needless to say the cost of the railway was high, not only in financial terms, costing £3.5 million, but more importantly in lost lives. The actual number of people who died owing to its construction will never be known as many men were only known by their 'nicknames' and were often buried on the open moorland in unmarked graves. A conservative estimate would put the number of fatalities well into four figures. Not only were they killed whilst working but also suffering an epidemic of smallpox probably caused from squalid living conditions.

The largest of the viaducts, the one you can see in the distance accounted for the lives of 108 men and a memorial to these workers can be seen at Chapel-le-Dale.
The Settle to Carlisle Railway was the last line to be constructed totally by hand, whilst dynamite, a new innovation for tunnel forging, was later used.

The line ran from St Pancras in London through the Midlands and Leeds to the north, but the 112 miles stretch from Leeds to Carlisle served few and called into question the validity of such a route. On the 11 August 1968 the last steam train, observed by thousands of enthusiasts, ran the line. Since then train lovers and public alike have constantly battled and succeeded in keeping the line open.

The S and C, as it is affectionately known is part of our national heritage and with grants available will surely remain preserved for many years to come.
If you have never travelled the line, make a date for an experience you will never forget.

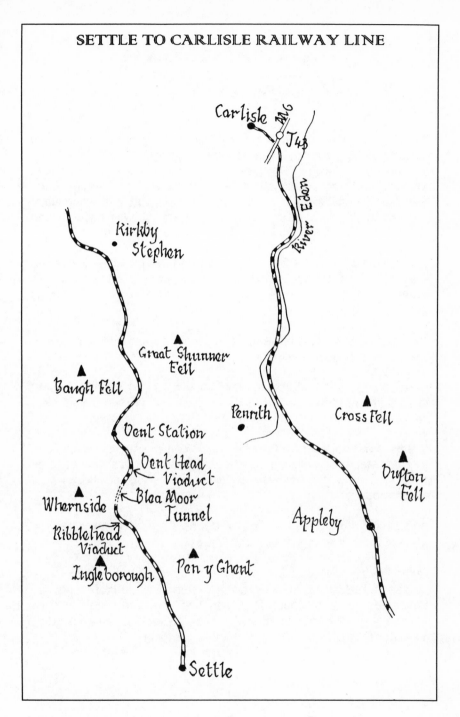

FAR GEARSTONES TO LEA YEAT
5.5 miles   MODERATE

On reaching the road turn left and continue along the road for a few hundred yards before joining a track from the right. This then leads to the houses at Winshaw. Pass the houses and continue along the path which at this point is steep and adjacent to the wall. At the summit the path bears right and the walk continues along an undulating path. Look to the right and you will see the route already covered and recognise Cam High Road.

The path now follows a fairly clear path up to High Gayle. Cross two stiles and continue towards Stoops Moss where the walker leaves North Yorkshire and enters Cumbria. The path is clear and easy to follow.

Crossing Stoops Moss in wet conditions can be hazardous, however, the walker soon joins the B6255 road.

On reaching the B6255 turn left and follow a lengthy stretch of road - three miles of tarmac which leads to **Lea Yeat (1).** Pass under the impressive Dent Head Viaduct and then alongside the River Dee.

If staying in Lea Yeat for the night and I can thoroughly recommend this, beware, as my walking companions Ken and Chris found to their cost - it is very easy to walk an extra mile or so looking for your accommodation.

If you have time to explore visit **St Johns Church, Cowgill (2)** and **The Quakers Meeting House, Lea Yeat (3).**

"Although this has been an arduous day, the feeling that night as we gorged ourselves in the Sportsman's Pub was one of euphoria." remarked Ken and Chris. They had just completed, not only the longest days walking ever attempted but also the most arduous within The Dales Way. They were now ready for anything.

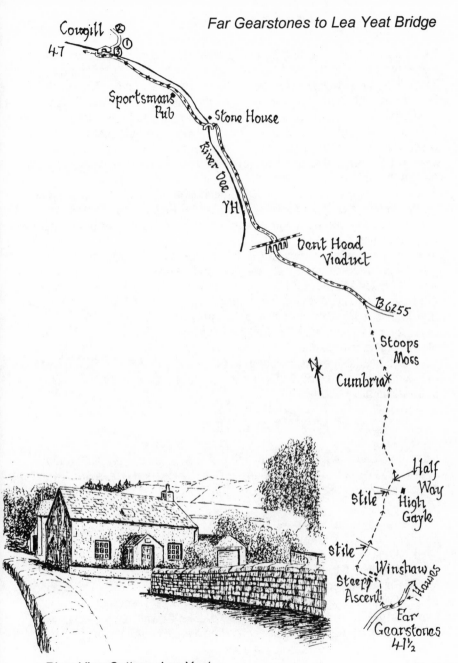

Cowgill

47

Sportsmans Pub

• Stone House

River Dee

YH

Dent Head Viaduct

B6255

Stoops Moss

Cumbria

Half Way

stile   High Gayle

stile

Winshaw

Steep Ascent   Hawes

Far Gearstones
41½

River View Cottage, Lea Yeat.

POINTS OF INTEREST

Lea Yeat (1). A welcoming hamlet at the end of a hard day and what better way to finish than with a nice cuppa. It was here that I found the most incredible facility adjacent to the bridge. Entering 'Tea In The Woodshed' at 3.30 p.m. on a Saturday afternoon not only was I desperate for a cuppa but also to find out how my beloved Newcastle United were doing at Elland Road. I was dumbfounded to be presented with a huge pot of tea and a radio. Incidentally we beat Leeds 1-0. Yet again the hospitality of the people along the route shines through.

St John's Church (2). Built in 1838 this delightful small church stands on the former site of a chapel erected by the Inghamites. Buried here are the bodies of many of the railway workers who perished during the construction of the Settle to Carlisle Railway.

The Quaker Meeting House (3). Right next to The Woodshed. The area was at the heart of Quakerism and even before George Fox arrived in Cowgill in 1652 there was a hard core of radical Yeomen in the Dales. Usually meetings were held in farm buildings but in 1701 a meeting house and burial ground were built at Cowgill, with one also being constructed at Dent.

The road next to the old meeting house leads to the highest railway station in England, Dent at approximately 350m.

FACILITIES

None until Lea Yeat, then a pub with excellent meals. Tea, coffee and snacks available next to the bridge in The Woodshed. Have you ever seen a sign like this?

ACCOMMODATION

Mr J Akrigg, Ewegales Farm, Cowgill, Nr Dent, Sedbergh, Cumbria. LA10 5RH. Tel: 01539 625440. Camp site only.

Mrs M Ferguson, Scow Cottage, Cowgill, Nr Dent, Sedbergh, Cumbria. LA10 5RN. Tel: 01539 625445. Well behaved dogs welcome.

Mr and Mrs Playfoot, River View, Lea Yeat, Nr Cowgill, Cumbria. LA10 5RF. Tel: 01539 625592. (Adjacent to Lea Yeat Bridge).

Without crossing the bridge bear left along the path towards Ewegales farm and camp site. On reaching the road bear left past the farm house until a gate is encountered on the left. Follow the path to Rivling Farm and with the buildings on the left pass through to enter a woodland at the stile. Continue along the pleasant tree lined walk only interrupted by the occasional stile.

On reaching Little Town the path is diverted over several stiles until meeting the access track. Cross straight over and head for the stile which leads back into the forestation. Continue until the path rises before ending at the stiles. A further access track is reached. Head upwards for a short distance before crossing to another stile on the right. Follow this path until yet another access track is reached. This time to Hackergill.

At Hackergill turn left and immediately right. The path is fairly well defined and leads to Laithbank where the access road leads back to the 'main' road. Turn left along the road and continue until passing a house on the left, where a gate to the right leads to Lenny's Leap and a return to the river, before crossing it at Nelly Bridge. Follow the river downstream, over more stiles before returning to the other bank at Tommy Bridge. After a short river bank walk head away from the river with the route climbing sharply before dropping to join the road at Mill Bridge. Turn right, crossing the bridge before taking the path to the right.

The next mile and a half provides a gentle comfortable walk alongside the river until reaching Church Bridge. Turn left and visit the lovely village of Dent. If not visiting Dent the route continues straight over at the bridge.

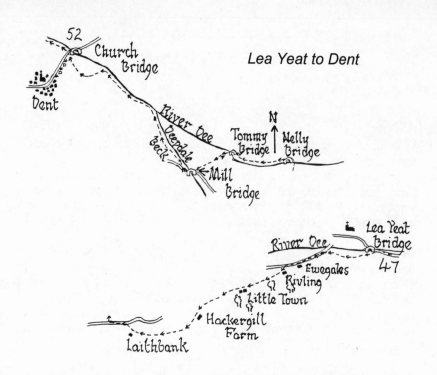

Lea Yeat to Dent

52
Church
Bridge
Dent
River Dee
Deepdale
Beck
Mill
Bridge
Tommy
Bridge
N
Nelly
Bridge
River Dee
Lea Yeat
Bridge
47
Ewegates
Rivling
Little Town
Hackergill
Farm
Laithbank

Approaching Dent village.

56

POINTS OF INTEREST

Dent. A detailed account of the folklore and history is found on the following pages.

FACILITIES

All amenities available in Dent. Shops, public telephone, pubs offering excellent meals and ale.

Dent Village

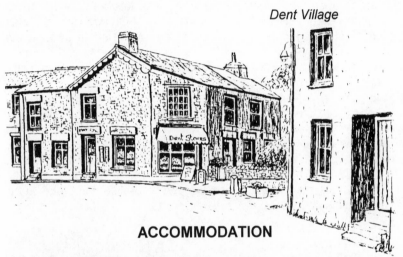

ACCOMMODATION

Mrs P M Allen, The White House, Flintergill, Dent, Cumbria. LA10 5QR. Tel: 015396 25041.
Mrs G Cheetham, Smithy Fold, Whernside, Dent, Sedbergh, Cumbria. LA10 5RE. Tel: 015396 25368.
E Johnson, Whernside Manor, Dent, Cumbria. LA10 5RE. Tel: 015396 25213. Bed and breakfast and bunk barn accommodation.
Mrs J A Newsham, Syke Fold, Dent, Sedbergh, Cumbria. LA10 5RE. Tel: 015396 25486. (Next to Whernside Cave Centre).
Mrs C Oversby, Low Hall, Dent, Sedbergh, Cumbria. LA10 5TD. Tel: 015396 25232.
Mrs A Priestley, Helmside View, The Laning, Dent, Sedbergh, Cumbria. LA10 5QY. Tel: 015396 25330.
Mrs J Underwood, Woman's Land Barn, Dent, Cumbria. LA10 5RE. Tel: 015396 25265.
Stone Close Tea Shop, Main Street, Dent, Cumbria. LA10 5QL. Tel: 015396 25231.

DENT ..... twinned with Transylvania?

The story begins long before Bram Stoker ever thought of his blood sucking Dracula. In fact 132 years before Stoker was born, back in 1715, when an old man of ninety four, George Hodgson died. For years before his death rumours abounded about the reasons for his longlevity. Was he in league with the Devil? Were his pointed molars evidence that he was in fact a vampire? Who is to say? But after his death several well respected Dalesfolk swore that they had seen him stalking through the moonlight. Many of those folk were said to meet an untimely death, so much so, that the body of George Hodgson was exhumed and buried by the church porch with a stake through his heart. It is said that when the coffin was opened the hair and the nails on the corpse were still growing and the flesh was still as pink as ever!

Folklore or fact? Whilst I strongly favour the former who can honestly say? Did Bram Stoker ever visit Dent? Was George the icon on which Dracula was based? If that is so then Stoker had the right idea to change his name - 'George Hodgson, Prince of Darkness' does not exactly have the same ring about it. The one certain fact is that George did exist and his gravestone rests beside the porch and still bears the hole supposedly drilled through it to allow the stake to be driven into his body.

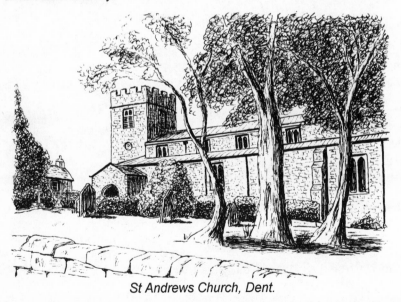

St Andrews Church, Dent.

On a more serious note Dent is an idyllic village, believed to have existed in Roman times. There is also evidence of a Norman presence with the church doorway at St Andrew's supporting a Norman arch. The original Grammar School's most famous attendant was Adam Sedgwick, a local boy, who went to Cambridge University and became one of the founders of the science we know today as Geology. Rather fittingly the memorial to Adam Sedgwick stands proudly in the heart of the village and is made from Shap granite.

Dent marble was a highly regarded stone coming in two forms, black and grey. It was black marble that was considered the finest and it was not until the introduction of cheap foreign imports that the Dent marble industry died.

Farming, needless to say, was then, as it is now, an important way of life and supplemented by knitting. The output of gloves and socks provided a very important income for the area. Knitting was done as much by the men as the women. On their way to the fields they would knit by holding one needle in their belts and one in their hand - an act hard to comprehend in modern society.

Dent is a haven and the folklore surrounding the vampire illustrates the character of the village which oozes out wherever you wander.

Explore the village and even make an overnight stop.

DENT TO MILLTHROP BRIDGE (Sedbergh)
5.5 miles   MODERATE

If you have visited Dent leave by the same route. Back to Church Bridge and a left turn leads down to the riverside path. This continues for almost a mile until a road is crossed by means of the stiles at Barth Bridge. Still remaining on the same side of the River Dee continue along this pleasant walk until a fence prior to Ellers Bridge. A path to the left leads to the road. Turn to the right and continue along the road for a mile and a half until meeting Rash Bridge.

Cross this and up to the main road where the route bears right towards the farm house on the right. Almost opposite take the gate on the left and a fairly distinct path leads quite severely uphill. At the top, cross the stile in the left hand corner of the field and make for the gate, which in turn leads onto a much wider bridleway and downhill towards Millthrop. This part of the route is rocky and can be hazardous - take great care.

On reaching the road bear right to the next junction where a left turn leads to the town of **Sedbergh (1)**, crossing **Millthrop Bridge (2)** in the process.

Ken and Chris on reaching Sedbergh were looking forward to a days rest. But as they said later this was the worst thing that they could have done. After the rest the next day proved tiresome and it was difficult to return to 'walking mode'. Far better to walk only a few miles just to keep the body active.

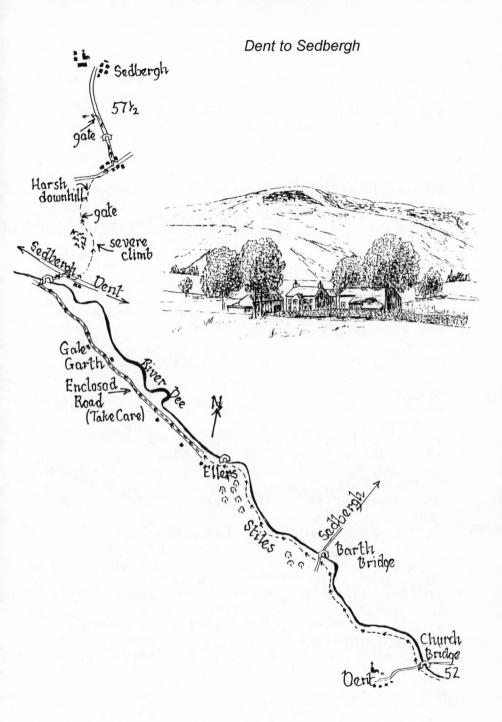

Sedbergh

57½

gate

Harsh
downhill

gate

severe
climb

Sedbergh   Dent

Gale
Garth

Enclosed
Road
(Take Care)

River Dee

N

Ellers

Stiles

Sedbergh

Barth
Bridge

Church
Bridge
52

Dent

POINTS OF INTEREST

Sedbergh (1). A pleasant market town. For more detailed description see page 64
Millthrop Bridge (2). The point at which the route turns left. However by continuing ahead the town of Sedbergh is visited..

FACILITIES

After leaving Dent there is nothing available until Sedbergh. As you would expect with a town the size of Sedbergh there are numerous, shops, cafes, pubs and hotels. I stayed at the Bull Hotel and found it comfortable with excellent staff and brimming with characters.

ACCOMMODATION

Gawthrop
Mrs Williamson, Ivy Dene, Gawthrop, Dent, Sedbergh, Cumbria. LA10 5TA. Tel: 015396 25353.
Dent Foot
Mrs A Hunter, Rash House, Dent Foot, Nr Sedbergh, Cumbria. LA10 5SU. Tel 015396 20113.
Sedbergh
Mr M Clark, Farfield Country Guest House, Hawes Road, Sedbergh, Cumbria. LA10 5LP. Tel: 015396 20537.
Mr J Handley, Catholes Farm, Sedbergh, Cumbria. LA10 5SS. Tel: 015396 20334.
Mrs J Jarvis, The Moss House, Garsdale Road, Sedbergh, Cumbria. LA10 5JL. Tel: 015396 20940.
Mrs A Jones, Yew Tree Cottage, 35 Loftus Hill, Sedbergh, Cumbria. LA10 5SQ. Tel: 015396 21600.
Mrs P Kerry, Marshall House, Main Street, Sedbergh, Cumbria. LA10 5BL. Tel: 015396 21053.
Mrs V Knowles, Pinfold Caravan Park, Garsdale Road, Sedbergh, Cumbria. LA10 5JL. Tel: 015396 20576. Camp site.
Mrs P Ramsden, Sun Lea, Joss Lane, Sedbergh, Cumbria. LA10 5AS. Tel: 015396 20828.
Mrs S Sharrocks, Holmecroft, Station Road, Sedbergh, Cumbria. LA10 5DW. Tel: 015396 20754.
Mr B Grahamslaw, Randall Hill, Station Road, Sedbergh, Cumbria. LA 10 5HJ. Tel: 015396 20633.

Mrs M Swainbank, 25 Bainbridge Road, Sedbergh, Cumbria. LA10 5AU. Tel: 015396 20685.
Miss M Thurlby, Stable Antiques, 15 Back Lane, Sedbergh, Cumbria. LA10 5AQ. Tel: 015396 20251
Mrs M Wilkinson, The Bull Hotel, Main Street, Sedbergh, Cumbria. LA10 5BL. Tel: 015396 20264.

The Bull Hotel, Main Street, Sedbergh.

SEDBERGH

Standing at the foot of the magnificent Howgill. A settlement has existed on the site of the modern market town Sedbergh since the 2nd century Roman occupation of Britain. The name Sedbergh is taken from 'Setberg' meaning a 'A Seat Shaped Hill'

Sedbergh has always been an important town. The Market Charter dates back to the 13th century, granted in 1251 during the reign of Henry III and the town has always provided a welcome halt for weary Pennine travellers. Even as a young boy in the 1950's I vividly remember the coach stopping here as it crossed the Pennines on its way from Newcastle to Blackpool.

The oldest part of the town is around the church and market place extending down the Main Street, which even today provides evidence of fabulous overhanging upper storeys - relics of the 17 century. The Church dedicated to St Andrew dates back to the Norman occupation and the arch for that period dominates the North entrance. The rounded arched nave and the chancel are 13th century.

As well as being a staging point for travellers Sedbergh's real claim to fame is its public school, founded in 1525 by Dr Roger Lupton. It survived the Dissolution to become a free Grammar School, from which the present complex is developed.

Over the years there have been a number of famous 'sons' of Sedbergh School. Adam Sedgwick from Dent and already mentioned attended, as did the mathematician John Dawson, scientist James Inman and in more recent years the most successful England Rugby Union Captain of all time - Will Carling.

Sedbergh is an interesting little town and well worth spending awhile exploring. Wherever you turn there are pockets of history awaiting your indulgence. Weavers Yard, a 17th century external chimney, which reputedly was one of the hiding places of Bonnie Prince Charlie as he retreated North during the 18th century. The Quaker Meeting House, the oldest in the North of England at nearby Brigflatts and dated 1675 at which George Fox, founder of the Quaker Movement preached.

Take the opportunity to stay awhile and enjoy an extended visit to Sedbergh.

SEDBERGH TO LINCOLN'S INN BRIDGE
3.75 miles   EASY

As The Dales Way crosses Millthrop Bridge it almost immediately leaves the road by the gate to the left. If you have visited Sedbergh then return by the same route almost to the bridge. The gate is now on your right. Walk into the small wood, pass through, leaving the gate to drop down to the banks of the River Rawthey.

Soon a small back lane is met. turn left and follow to its end at Birks Mill. The route returns to the river bank and remains in close proximity, crossing the disused railway line to arrive at **Brigflatts (1).** After passing the farm the river bears to the left whilst the path continues up to join the main A683 road.

Turn left at the road and walk for a good half mile before joining a footpath to the right. Be careful along this section. Although the footpath is marked by a guidepost it is still partially hidden by the roadside bushes.

Follow the path, crossing a stream before rising to the fence. Follow this to the far corner of the field and then to the right which leads to a gate and then left to the cottages at High Oaks.

Again be careful, the path required leads to the right just after the farmhouse. As this track ends at the gate, turn right and continue to the next gate, whereupon a wide track leads to Luneside Farm. After passing the buildings leave the track at the gate on the left. Hugging the fence, proceed to the stile before joining the River Lune which leads directly to **Lincoln's Inn Bridge (2).**

High Oaks

POINTS OF INTEREST

Brigflatts (1). As previously mentioned in the history of Sedbergh the oldest Quaker Meeting House in England can be found at Brigflatts. Built in 1675 George Fox, the founder of Quakerism is known to have preached here. The house is located just off the path beyond the farm buildings.

Lincoln's Inn Bridge (2). Although the name seems to suggest a welcoming water hole I am sorry to be the bearer of bad tidings. Whilst there was once an inn here it ceased to exist many years ago. One look at the bridge seems to suggest that the workers constructing it spent many hours in the pub. What happened to symmetrical arches?

FACILITIES

None.

ACCOMMODATION

None.

LINCOLN INN'S BRIDGE TO CROOK OF LUNE BRIDGE   3.5 miles EASY

From the bridge cross the A684 road to a gate and once again follow the path alongside the river. Within minutes the impressive arches of the **Lune Viaduct (1)** appear. Pass through the arches and the path then begins to veer off to the right, uphill and away from the river, until meeting a stile which leads to the track down to Low Branthwaite.

On reaching the access track at Low Branthwaite cross straight over before bearing left alongside the fence, until a gentle climb leads to an enclosed way. At the end of the enclosure take the stile to the left of the access track, passing the farm, before descending to a small barn, where the track leads to Nether Bainbridge Farm.

At the farm, take the stile before the barn to your left and, passing the barn turn left again. At the gate take the short climb before descending to another farm - Hole House.

Enter the farmyard and pass between the houses to a gate at the far end. At the footbridge cross Smithy Beck stream and take the low path to rejoin the river. This peaceful and quiet riverside amble leads to another footbridge near Thwaite farm.

Continue alongside the river until reaching the gate below Crook of Lune Farm to your right. Follow the track which in turn leads to a narrow lane leading down to the **Crook of Lune Bridge (2).**

Crook of Lune Bridge
→ Howgill   64¾
• Crook Farm

Hole House Farm

Nether Bainbridge Farm

Low Branthwaite Farm

←The Lune Viaduct

Lincoln's Inn Bridge 61¼

POINTS OF INTEREST

The Lune Viaduct (1). This magnificent structure towering above the peaceful countryside is built from red sandstone and once carried the Ingleton to Tebay Railway - alas no longer with us.

The Crook of Lune Bridge (2). Much more impressive than the bridge at Lincoln's Inn. This thankfully little used bridge provides an idyllic spot for a short break from the walk.

Until the county boundary changes were implemented in 1974 the bridge marked the border between Westmorland and the West Riding of Yorkshire. Today the bridge marks the end of The Dales National Park.

FACILITIES

None in this section.

ACCOMMODATION

Whilst there is no Dales Way listed accommodation on this stretch there is accommodation available within half a mile past the Crook of Lune Bridge.

68

CROOK OF LUNE BRIDGE TO GRAYRIGG
5.0 miles MODERATE

From the bridge continue along the lane passing the houses and then climb the road past Lowgill Viaduct to the junction.

Turn right and then left continuing for a short while along the road until Half Island House on the left. Leave the road and walk along the path in front of the house. This rises fairly steeply to a stile and by now the heavy volume of traffic on the **M6 Motorway (1)** will probably be thundering in your ears. At the stile continue straight ahead along the path to a track which appears to lead to Lakethwaite Farm. Take the track but almost immediately go over the stile to the right. Continue past the farm, over several stiles until reaching a quiet back road. Almost opposite is a stile, the path leading to the farm bridge which crosses the motorway.

After the bridge turn immediately left and pass the farm buildings where a stile leads onto a narrow road. Turn left and as the road widens leave it by the gate on the right. Again, over several stiles, before reaching a gate which leads to a drive and to the right of Holme Park Farm.

The route is now fairly obvious until Moresdale Hall is reached. Continue passing the first house, cross the bridge and instead of following the drive bear right up the hill. A further drive appears with the Hall on your right. Cross over the drive walking through the trees before crossing a beck and emerging at a stile leading to a lane.

Turn left along the lane and at the junction turn sharp right. Within yards there is a **choice of route (2)**. If staying at **Grayrigg (3)** continue along the road to the main road and village. If, however, you are continuing along the walk, turn left opposite the solitary building and refer to the next section.

Half Island House

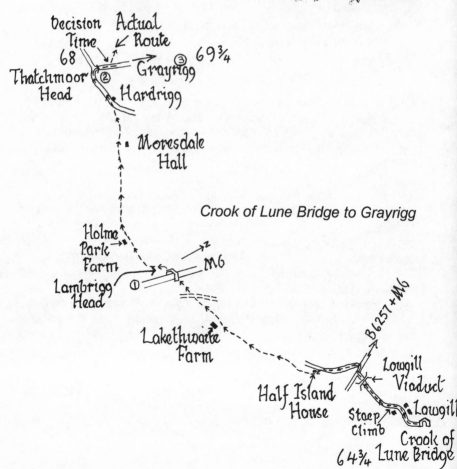

Decision Time 68 Actual Route

Thatchmoor Head ② ③ Grayrigg 69¾

Hardrigg

Moresdale Hall

Crook of Lune Bridge to Grayrigg

Holme Park Farm

M6

Lambrigg Head ①

Lakethwaite Farm

B6257 + M6

Half Island House

Lowgill Viaduct

Steep Climb

Lowgill

Crook of Lune Bridge 64¾

POINTS OF INTEREST

M6 Motorway (1). An unusual subject to have as a point of interest. However, if like me after days and days of peaceful solitude you are horrified at the appearance of such an eyesore and treat it with the contempt it deserves, just stop and think for a while. Whilst we all love the rural surroundings as our playground, many people live here and road communications are vital to the prosperity of the region. Quite simply the M6 is a necessity.

Choice of Route (2). On reaching the junction at Thatchmoor Head there is a choice. If you are staying in Grayrigg, then continue along the road to the village. There is no need to return to this point to resume the walk as a short walk down the A685 will return you to the route. The strip map will help.

Grayrigg (3). An exceptionally sleepy hamlet.

FACILITIES

No shops but there is a public telephone in Grayrigg.

ACCOMMODATION

Mr & Mrs Hogg, Tarnclose, Beckfoot, Lowgill, Near Kendal, Cumbria. LA8 0BL. Tel: 01539 824658.

Mrs Bindloss, Grayrigg Hall, Grayrigg, Near Kendal, Cumbria. LA8 9BU. Tel: 01539 824689.

Mrs Boardley, Holme Park Hall, Lambrigg, Near Kendal, Cumbria. LA8 0DS. Tel: 01539 824336. (First house after crossing the M6).

Mrs Johnson, Punchbowl House, Grayrigg, Near Kendal, Cumbria. LA8 9BU. Tel: 01539 824345.

Mrs Knowles, Myers Farm, Docker, Grayrigg, Near Kendal, Cumbria. LA8 0DF. Tel: 01539 824610.

Mrs Sanderson, High Barn, Shaw End, Patton, Near Kendal, Cumbria. LA8 9DU. Tel: 01539 824625. (The Dales Way passes through the garden).

Diversionary Route. This route applies if you have visited the village of Grayrigg. From the junction in the village, face the church and turn left following the A685 towards Kendal, Go past Ghyll Bank and a little further down the road take the footpath off to your right. Here you rejoin the original route on the access track to Thursgill.

Original Route. On reaching the junction at Thatchmoor Head turn sharp right and immediately left onto the footpath opposite the building. Follow the path across the field before crossing the railway line at the gate. Take care - this is a busy line. Walking directly away from the line will soon bring you to Green Head Farm. Keep the building on your right and follow the access track. Just before the cattle grid turn right and once over the footbridge pass through the gate between the farm buildings and out to the A685. Turn right for a few yards before crossing and taking the access track for Thursgill.

Cross the beck and through the gate on the left. Continue over several stiles until the route surmounts the crest of the rise and arrives at a track. Turn right towards the barn and continue through a gate in the hedge facing you. Cross over the footbridge and walk uphill to a gate leading into a lane. Turn right and at the second gate on the left a path runs parallel with the road. Take this path to the left which leads through a house yard before rising to meet the road. Cross the road and follow the driveway to Biglands, turning left before the house to a stile, which then leads over further stiles to **Black Moss Tarn (1).**

From the tarn head for the pylon before dropping down to New House Farm. Enter the yard and then turn left to the gate, which gives a pleasant walk to the access road for Goodham Scales. Turn left and on reaching the bend take the gate in front to follow another road down to Garnett Folds. Continue towards the A6.

At the A6, turn left and after a few yards cross the road and walk up the drive for Burton House. A waymarker shows the route through the gate on the left, followed by another immediately afterwards. At this point on the route The Dales Way is well marked and leads to the road junction prior to Oakbank. At the road turn sharp right and just before

72

the row of houses on the right a gate to the left leads back into the countryside. Cross over the stile and make for the River Sprint. Left past the bridge, cross the stile and join the road at Sprint Bridge.

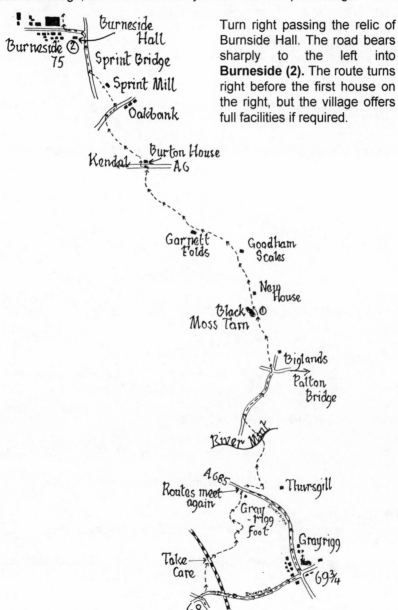

Turn right passing the relic of Burnside Hall. The road bears sharply to the left into **Burneside (2).** The route turns right before the first house on the right, but the village offers full facilities if required.

POINTS OF INTEREST

Black Moss Tarn (1). Nothing spectacular about this expanse of water, although it does provide a pleasant stop. On a wet blustery day I decided on a short break, sheltering with my back to the north side of a wall. Whilst hearing the farmer working with his tractor in the field behind me I never thought he would be muck spreading. Alas it was too late. I was covered from head to foot in farmyard delights and really needed the tarn to get clean!!

Burneside (2). Approaching this thriving community your first sight is the Mill. A rather ugly building but nevertheless an important source of industry for the village. For the best part of a century the mill has enabled the village to flourish and provide reasonable financial security for its inhabitants.

FACILITIES

Burneside offers all the facilities you would expect. A small supermarket, public telephone and The Jolly Anglers Pub.

ACCOMMODATION

Mrs Crawford, The Honey Pot, Tarn Bank, Skelsmergh, Kendal, Cumbria. Tel: 01539 823288. (Refreshments available during the day).

Mrs Finn, Edge Bank Farmhouse, Skelsmergh, Kendal, Cumbria. LA8 9AS. Tel: 01539 823218.

Camping and Caravan Club Site, Millcrest, Shap Road, Skelsmergh, Kendal, Cumbria. LA9 6NY. Tel: 01539 741363. Camp site only.

Mrs Metcalfe, Hollin Root Farm, Garth Row, Skelsmergh, Kendal, Cumbria. LA8 9AW. Tel 01539 823638.

Kendal

Mrs Brindley, Bridge House, 65 Castle Street, Kendal, Cumbria. LA9 7AD. Tel: 01539 722041.

Mrs Paylor, Fairways, 102 Windermere Road, Kendal, Cumbria. LA9 5EZ. Tel: 01539 725564.

Burneside

Mrs C J Gregg, Jolly Anglers Inn, Burneside, Kendal, Cumbria. LA9 5QS. Tel: 01539 732552.

Mrs C J Gregg, Strickland Ketel Guest House, 1 Ketel Houses, Burneside, Kendal, Cumbria. LA9 9HG. Tel: 10539 729324.

Sprint Mill

BURNESIDE TO STAVELEY
3.5 miles EASY

If you have replenished stocks in Burneside leave by the same route as you entered, turning left past the house at the gate. If you have not been into the village turn right immediately before the first house.

Follow the path to skirt the perimeter of the factory to meet the River Kent. Continue along the river until Bowston Bridge. Cross the bridge and proceed along the lane and turn right on meeting the road. This leads into **Bowston (1)**. A path leads off to the right past a delightful cottage and the walk then rejoins the river. Continue along the river until meeting a surfaced lane leading to the new development at Cowens Head.

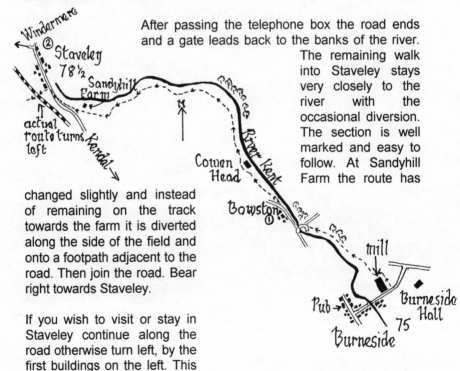

After passing the telephone box the road ends and a gate leads back to the banks of the river. The remaining walk into Staveley stays very closely to the river with the occasional diversion. The section is well marked and easy to follow. At Sandyhill Farm the route has changed slightly and instead of remaining on the track towards the farm it is diverted along the side of the field and onto a footpath adjacent to the road. Then join the road. Bear right towards Staveley.

If you wish to visit or stay in Staveley continue along the road otherwise turn left, by the first buildings on the left. This leads along a track and under the railway line.

POINTS OF INTEREST

Bowston (1). Whilst Bowston is a very small and pleasant village the cottage already mentioned and prior to leaving the road is an incredible sight. The garden contains hundreds of ornaments from dinosaurs to mermaids, gnomes to crocodiles and all accompanied by messages to walkers. As you pass the garden, appears the crowning glory - a sign which reads:

"Dales Way, To All Walkers, Hikers and Ramblers. Have a nice day".

Superb. Even after 80 miles I never cease to be amazed by the people along The Dales Way. A wonderful experience and thank you to the couple in the cottage.

Staveley (2). See page 78

FACILITIES

Staveley offers good facilities including pubs, shops, post office, public telephone and accommodation. Staveley is the last stop before Bowness.

ACCOMMODATION

Bowston
Mrs J Jamieson, Kent Dene, Bowston, Kendal, Cumbria. LA8 9HG. Tel: 01539 724929.
Staveley
Mrs A Crawford, 17 Danes Road, Staveley, Near Kendal, Cumbria. LA9 9PW. Tel: 01539 821148.
Mrs B Fishwick, Stock Bridge Farm, Kendal Road, Staveley, Cumbria. LA8 9LP. Tel: 01539 821580.
Mr & Mrs Kelly, Fell View, 12a Danes Road, Staveley, Cumbria. LA8 9PW. Tel: 01539 821209.
Alan & Lyn McCuaig, The Eagle and Child, Kendal Road, Staveley, Cumbria. LA8 9LP. Tel: 01539 821320.

STAVELEY

Situated close to Kendal it is difficult to imagine how tourism seems to have eluded this village. Whilst The Lake District National Park is inundated with worldwide visitations, for some unknown reason Staveley is one of the lesser known settlements, although it is steeped in its own history and well worth exploring.

Standing on the northern bank of the River Kent with the River Gowan running through the centre, Staveley was founded as far back as the 13th century. The roaring strength of the River Kent, reputedly the fastest flowing river in England, made this an idea site for the creation of water powered mills, used for the cleaning of woollen cloth spun in the area.

During the following four centuries Staveley had more than its fair share of strife and plague and there was the constant threat from marauding Scots. Even so the village continued to grow and by the turn of the 18th century there were over a dozen mills in the immediate area. Whilst wool was always the premier commodity a cotton mill was also introduced. However, the remoteness of Staveley proved to be an unsurmountable obstacle, cotton was not a success and a return to the woollen industry was inevitable. With it came the manufacture of Staveley's most famous product the Bobbin.

The prosperity of Staveley continued to thrive and by the turn of the 20th century there were almost a thousand inhabitants.

Unfortunately, the progress of time, cheaper imports, the diminishing of certain commodities and the collapse of the textile industry led to the collapse of Staveley's industrial security. However it still remains a pleasant and welcome break for the walker or motorist.

The Staveley and District History Society have designed a walk with accompanying booklet starting from Staveley's oldest building, St Margaret's Church (circa 1338) to give the visitor an in depth guide around the village. Worth considering to help you explore Staveley.

St Margaret's Church, Staveley.

The Duke William, Staveley.

Having passed under the railway line follow the track which bears to the right. At the end of the field follow the line of the wall to the left which leads to Moss Side, crossing the stile to gain access to the drive.

Follow the drive until meeting the road and cross the fly over. Soon the road is left by turning right into Field Close.

Once at the top, turn left through the gate passing along the field with a copse on your left. This leads to a quiet back road, turn right and take a fairly steep climb which ultimately gives a superb view of the heart of **Lakeland (1).** The route now drops down to reach the junction prior to Fell Plain Farm.

Turn right at the junction and begin another climb. As the summit is reached a path to the left leads up between the walls. Within a few hundred yards the track ends at a gate. Pass through the gate and continue in the same direction to a further gate which in turn leads past another copse to your right. At the bottom leave the track and follow a small stream down to a gate and then a stile before joining a track to Crag House Farm.

In front of the barn take the track to the right towards the farmhouse, soon leaving it to the right. Go through the gate to a road at Outrun Nook. Turn right and very soon left along a track to Hag End farm.

Approaching New Hall Farm.

POINTS OF INTEREST

The heart of Lakeland (1). As the summit is reached past New Hall Farm the imposing summits of England's highest mountains, Scafell Pike and the incomparable Great Gable can be seen in the distance - weather permitting!!

FACILITIES

None in this section.

ACCOMMODATION

There is no Dales Way Association listed accommodation between Staveley and Bowness.

HAG END FARM TO BOWNESS
3.25 miles   EASY

Pass between the buildings at Hag End before turning left alongside the remnants of a wall. Cross at the far end and make for the stile in the next wall. The track now rises to meet two gates in quick succession before descending to join a track. Continue to the junction and then turn left passing Cleabarrow before arriving at the junction with the B5284.

Turn right along the road and after about 80 yards take the road to the right making for Low Cleabarrow. Prior to reaching the buildings turn left through a gate, descending through two more gates, before a short rise through the trees to two further gates.

Cross straight over the road and head downhill past Matson Ground until reaching a further road. Again straight over and through a series of further gates leading to a path. Continue until meeting the next road. Turn right and after a few yards bear left to a path. Continue across the field before turning left through a gate and on to meet the farm road. Cross the road following the path down the field. Over another track before the first glimpse of **Windermere (1).** From here you only have a short walk to reach **The Dales Way Seat (2)** and the official finishing line!! Having achieved your goal take all the time you need to milk in the immense satisfaction that you will undoubtedly feel.

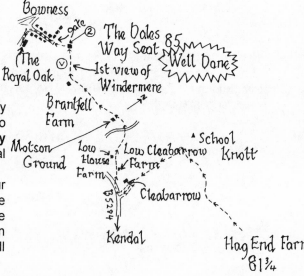

POINTS OF INTEREST

Windermere (1). The largest and most visited lake in England and providing a fitting finale to The Dales Way.
The Dales way Seat (2). This was built to mark the official end of The Dales Way or the beginning if you prefer the reverse route. Over the coming years further seats will appear along the route.

FACILITIES

Bowness is one of the most popular towns within the Lake District and there are all the facilities that you would expect of a popular tourist town.

ACCOMMODATION

Bowness
Mrs R Erwig, 2 Annisgarth House, Annisgarth Avenue, Bowness, Cumbria. LA23 2HF. Tel: 015394 48049.
Anne & Ernie Fallowfield, Overthere, Brantfell Road, Bowness, Cumbria. LA23 3AE. Tel: 015394 46412.
Mr G Fanstone, Deloraine, Helm Road, Bowness, Cumbria. LA23 2HS. Tel: 015394 45557.
Mrs P Granger, Holmlea, Kendal Road, Bowness, Cumbria. LA23 3EW. Tel: 015394 42597.
Mrs R Holliday, Gillercombe, 97 Craig Walk, Bowness, Cumbria. LA23 2JS. Tel: 015394 45928.
Mr R Hood, Fairfield Hotel, Brantfell Road, Bowness, Cumbria. LA23 3AE. Tel: 01539 446565.
D Kelso, Laurel Cottage, St Martins Square, Bowness, Cumbria. LA23 3EF. Tel: 015394 45594.
Lyndhurst, 101 Craig Walk, Bowness, Cumbria. LA23 2JS. Tel: 015394 44304.
Mr F Sanderson, Blenheim Lodge, Brantfell Road, Bowness, Cumbria. LA23 3AE. Tel: 015394 43440.
Mr J Tomlinson, Bowfell Cottage, Middle Entrance Drive, Storrs Park, Bowness, Cumbria. LA23 3JY. Tel: 015394 44835. (Situated 1 mile south of Bowness).
White Lodge Hotel, Lake Road, Bowness, Cumbria. LA23 2JJ. Tel: 015394 43624.
Mrs J Whitfield, Eastbourne Hotel, Biskey Howe Road, Bowness, Cumbria. LA23 2JR. Tel: 015394 43525.

Windermere (1 mile north of Bowness)

Gill & Barry Pearson, Broadlands Guest House, 19 Broad Street, Windermere, Cumbria. LA23 2AB. Tel: 015394 46532.

Mrs E Shore, Merebeck, 8 College Road, Windermere, Cumbria. LA23 1BX. Tel: 015394 45881.

The Royal Oak, Bowness.

The Centre of Bowness.

BOWNESS-ON-WINDERMERE

Standing on the eastern shore of England's largest lake the small town of Bowness has been a popular tourist attraction for more than a century.

The Victorians flocked here in their thousands to take the steam boat trips up the lake to Ambleside and back, bringing with it a town which relies almost entirely on tourism and to that extent the place is a total success, being without doubt one of the busiest towns in the Lake District.

Whilst Bowness is a haven for the day-tripper it has somewhat unfairly been regarded by experienced hikers as a place to avoid. The mass of shops and throngs of people are not what the walker is looking for, however, Bowness does provide a pleasant place to stay overnight after the rigours of the walk. A chance perhaps to sample some of the many fine restaurants.

Historically Bowness has many places to visit and these include St Martin's Church, the Steamboat Museum and the Beatrix Potter Museums.

The town is an excellent base for exploring the hills of the Southern Lakeland with pleasure boats providing regular trips including a service to Ambleside.
The Parklands Country Club provides excellent recuperation with swimming pools, sauna and Jacuzzi facilities. The Royal Oak is a fine pub with a superb menu, well kept ales and a friendly atmosphere, which encaptures the whole spirit found along the length of The Dales Way.

REFLECTIONS

Now that you have completed The Dales Way and finally vacated The Dales Way Seat allow me to relate further directions for another half mile .... from the seat continue down hill to the gate which exits at the top of Brantfell Road. Follow the steep road down and into the centre of Bowness. A left turn will lead you to The Royal Oak, purchase a pint and toast yourself in what I regard as the finishing pub to this magnificent walk.

A time for reflection .... At the end of every long distance walk the thoughts and the pleasures of the walker are a totally individual experience. Many feel initial elation after completing, what is after all, a memorable achievement, followed perhaps by a tinge of sadness that the adventure is finally over.

What I say to you is, it is not over, it is only the beginning. There are many more adventures waiting for you. By walking The Dales Way you have proved that you are an accomplished hiker. Demanding walks beckon throughout the UK and you can tackle any of them with confidence.

Whilst this walk is an individual experience I hope that I have been able to guide you through some of the history and lesser known facts about the regions of The Dales Way. It truly is a memorable trek and I am sure that you really have had **Seven Glorious Days** or even perhaps longer.

TRIBUTE

At the outset of this book I included the comments of two 'strangers' I met on the riverside at Barden Tower, Ken and Chris who were attempting their first ever long distance walk. Having left them at Sedbergh I never saw them again .... until they came down that slope to The Dales Seat, just five hours after I had. The emotion of that day will live with us forever. Their achievement was second to none and I am privileged to be able to call them friends.

So after many highs and a number of lows, would they continue with their new found hobby? Amazingly it was already in the planning stage. In just eight months time they would be departing St Bees Head for Robin Hoods Bay - 190 miles of 'The Coast to Coast'.

Without the many people who give their time so generously to help maintain the footpaths of England, walks such as The Dales Way would fall into obscurity. All too often these walks are taken for granted, but it takes a vast amount of time and money to continually preserve them. Men like Colin Speakman (Chairman) and David Smith (Secretary) are shining examples of the hard working body of people who are collectively known as **"The Dales Way Association"**. On behalf of walkers everywhere I thank them and pay tribute to them.

As you read this remember that you can help to preserve The Dales Way by becoming a member of the Association.

INDEX

Accidents 8
Accommodation 11, 14, 17, 20,
25, 29, 32, 35, 37, 40, 44, 46,
48, 54, 57, 62, 66, 68, 71, 74,
77, 81, 83
Addingham12, 15, 16, 17, 18
Appletreewick 12, 26, 27, 28,
29

Barden Bridge 12, 24, 27
Barden Tower 23, 24, 25
Beatrix Potter 85
Beckermonds 43, 44
Birks Mill 65
Black Moss Tarn 72, 74
Blea Moor Tunnel 49, 50, 51
Bolton Abbey 2, 19, 20
Bolton Bridge 19, 20, 23, 26
Bolton Hall 19, 20
Bolton Priory 12, 18, 19, 20, 21,
22, 23
Bowness-on-Windermere 1, 12,
82, 83, 84, 85
Bowston 76, 77
Brigflatts 65, 66
Buckden 38, 40, 45
Burneside 12, 72, 73, 74, 76
Burnsall 12, 26, 27, 28, 29, 30
Burton House 73

Cam High Road 47, 48, 52
Cam Houses 12, 45, 46, 47
Church Bridge, Dent 55, 56
Churches
    St Andrew's, Dent 58, 59
    St Andrew's, Sedbergh 64
    St John's, Appletr'wick 28
    St John's, Cowgill 52, 54

St Martin's, Bowness 85
St Michael's, Hub'holme
39, 41
St Michael's, Linton 30,
31
St Peter's, Addingham
15, 16, 17
Cleabarrow 82
Compass work 6
Conistone Pie 33, 34, 35, 36
Cowen's Head 76
Cowgill 52
Crag House Farm 80
Crook of Lune 67, 68, 69, 70

Dales Way Seat 82, 83, 85
Deepdale 43
Dent 12, 55, 56, 57, 58, 59, 60,
61
Dent Head Viaduct 51, 53
Dent Station 51

Ellers Bridge 61
Equipment 5
Ewegales Farm 56

Far Gearstones 47, 52, 53
Fell Plain Farm 80
Field Close 80
Foreword 1

Garnett Folds 72, 73
Grassington 12, 30, 31, 32, 33,
34
Grayrigg 12, 69, 70, 71, 72, 73

Hag End Farm 80, 82

88

Half Island House 70
High Gayle 53
High Oaks 65, 66
Hole House Farm 67
Howgill Fells 61
Hubberholme 38, 39, 40, 41,
42, 43

Ilkley 1, 12, 13, 14, 15, 16, 17

Kettlewell 12, 36, 37, 38, 39

Lea Green 33, 35
Lea Yeat 52, 53, 54, 55
Lincoln's Inn Bridge 65, 66, 67
Linton 32
Linton Falls12, 30
Loup Scar 30
Low Braithwaite 67
Lowgill 70
Lune Viaduct 67, 68

Map Work 6
Matson Ground 82
Millthrop Bridge 60, 61, 62
Mock Beggar Hall 28
Moresdale Hall 70
Moss Side 73, 80
M6 Motorway 69, 70, 71

Nelly's Bridge 55, 56
Nether Bainbridge 67
Nethergill 45

Olicana 13, 18, 19
Ordnance Survey 6
Oughtershaw 43, 45
Outrun Nook 80, 81

Pennine Way 47, 48

Planning 9, 11
Pubs
    Blue Bell, Kettlewell 37
    Buck Inn, Buckden 40
    Bull Hotel, Sedbergh 63
    Craven Arms, Appl'wick
    26
    Fox & Hounds, Starbotton
    38
    George Inn, Hubb'holme
    42
    Jolly Anglers, Burneside
    74
    Kings Head, Kettlewell 37
    New Inn, Appl'wick 29
    Racehorses, Kettlewell 38
    Red Lion, Burnsall 30
    Royal Oak, Bowness 82
    Sportsman, Lea Yeat 53

Quaker Meeting House 52, 54,
66, 64

Railway, Settle to Carlisle 49,
50, 51
Reducing Risks 8
Ribblehead Viaduct 47, 49, 51

Safety 67
Sandyhill Farm 76
Scargill House 36
Sedbergh 12, 60, 61, 62, 63.
64, 65
Sedgewick, Adam 64
Sprint Mill 73, 75
Starbotton 38, 39
Staveley 12, 76, 77, 78, 80
Steamboat Museum 85
Stoops Moss 53
Strid Wood 24
Swarthgill 45

Thatchmoor Head 70, 72
Tommy's Bridge 55, 56

Walking Attire 6
Windermere Lake 76, 82, 83
Winshaw 53
Woodshed, Lea Yeat 54

Yockenthwaite 43, 44
Yorkshire Three Peaks 47, 48